Hickory Furniture Mart

A LANDMARK HISTORY

60 YEARS OF MARKET DEVELOPMENT

Other books from Redhawk Publications:

Birdhouse by Clayton Joe Young and Tim Peeler
Bouquets Hadn't Been Invented Yet by Tony Deal
Food Culture Recipes from the Henry River Mill Village
From Darkness: The Fated Soules Series, Book One by Jan Lindie
Going To Wings by Sandra Worsham
Hickory: Then & Now by Richard Eller and Tammy Panther
Hickory: Then & Now The Complete Texts by Richard Eller
Hickory: Then & Now The Complete Photograph Collection
What Came to Me—Collected Columns Vol One by Arlene Neal
More by Shelby Stephenson
Mother Lover Child & Me by Erin Anthony
Newton: Then & Now by Richard Eller and Sylvia Kidd Ray
Piedmont The Jazz Rat Of Cunningham Park by Mike Bruner
A Place Where Trees had Names by Les Brown
Polio, Pitchforks & Perseverance by Richard Eller
Sanctuary Art Journal 2018, 2019, 2020
Secrets I'm Dying to Tell You by Terry Barr
Sittin' In with the Sun by Carter Monroe
Sleeping Through the Graveyard Shift by Al Maginnes
The Legends of Harper House - The Shuler Era by Richard Eller
Waffle House Blues by Carter Monroe
We Might As Well Eat by Terry Barr
We See What We Want to See: The Henry River Mill Village in Poetry, Photography, and History by Clayton Joe Young and Tim Peeler
Win/Win by G. Leroy Lail

Hickory Furniture Mart

A LANDMARK HISTORY

60 YEARS OF MARKET DEVELOPMENT

G. LEROY LAIL

RICHARD ELLER

REDHAWK PUBLICATIONS

Copyright©2020 by Leroy Lail

All rights reserved. No part of this publication may be reproduced, distributed, or transmitted in any form or by any means, including photocopying, recording, or other electronic or mechanical methods, without the prior written permission of the publisher, except in the case of brief quotations embodied in critical reviews and certain other noncommercial uses permitted by copyright law. For permission requests, write to the publisher, addressed "Attention: Permissions Coordinator," at the address below.

Redhawk Publications
2550 US Hwy 70 SE
Hickory, NC 28602

Robert Canipe, Publisher and Editor-in-Chief rcanipe@cvcc.edu

Ordering Information:
Quantity sales. Special discounts are available on quantity purchases by corporations, associations, and others. For details, contact the publisher at the address or email above.

ISBN: 978-1-952485-12-1

Hickory Furniture Mart

A LANDMARK HISTORY

60 YEARS OF MARKET DEVELOPMENT

G. LEROY LAIL

RICHARD ELLER

REDHAWK
PUBLICATIONS

Copyright©2020 by Leroy Lail

All rights reserved. No part of this publication may be reproduced, distributed, or transmitted in any form or by any means, including photocopying, recording, or other electronic or mechanical methods, without the prior written permission of the publisher, except in the case of brief quotations embodied in critical reviews and certain other noncommercial uses permitted by copyright law. For permission requests, write to the publisher, addressed "Attention: Permissions Coordinator," at the address below.

Redhawk Publications
2550 US Hwy 70 SE
Hickory, NC 28602

Robert Canipe, Publisher and Editor-in-Chief rcanipe@cvcc.edu

Ordering Information:
Quantity sales. Special discounts are available on quantity purchases by corporations, associations, and others. For details, contact the publisher at the address or email above.

ISBN: 978-1-952485-12-1

"Furniture is a competitive business, Southern furniture manufacturers will tell you. So it is when it comes to the business of selling furniture."[1]—Robert Marks Furniture Reporter, April 1966

In 1965, the Furniture Factories Marketing Association attempted to corral both the High Point and Hickory markets into opening at the same time in order to give no buyer an advantage on the new styles. Instead of encompassing two weekends by starting early and finishing late, the group of manufacturers in the association, set a firm April Monday morning in 1965 as the start of the spring market. High Point adhered. Both the Hickory Furniture Mart and the Hickory Home Furnishings Mart, stayed with the old schedule.

Business was just too good. It was not in the interest of either makers or sellers to deprive furniture retailers from seeing the new lines and promptly placing their orders just to adhere to an organization that could be argued, favored the High Point manufacturers. "Plants in the Hickory area have been operating on full production schedules, with order backlogs from six to eight weeks in hand, said Robert Marks. He

---

[1] Robert Marks, "For Furniture Marketing, New Air of Cooperation," High Point Enterprise, April 22, 1966, p. 18.

added, "so critical is the shortage of skilled labor that manufacturers - although they do not admit it openly - have been pirating workers from each other."[2] The owners of Broyhill, Bernhardt, Century, Drexel, Hickory Chair and Henredon had never seen such days.

Times were good for their competition too. Expansion was in the works for almost every furniture manufacturer. Looking up the road from High Point, observers noted, "Hickory Tavern Furniture Co. has completed construction of a new manufacturing plant. Century Furniture Co. has opened a new plant that utilizes conveyor belts, automation and computers to speed production."[3] To meet the demand, companies were trying to stay ahead of buying interests. Marks noted, "Almost all manufacturers are introducing new lines at the market. The new furniture is priced in line with production costs, which, manufacturers declared, are rising steadily. 'I suppose you could call it inflation,' one commented."[4]

Peacetime prosperity in the United States continued unabated in the fall of 1965 with consumer interest in new styles, more modern and worldly, a part of their appetite. "In styling, the Spanish influence appears strongly in the new furniture. Upholstered furniture is acquiring a richer, more plush look, particularly in the Early American and Country Italian and French patterns. Velvet seems to be the new favorite in fabrics."[5] It was no longer sufficient to provide a table and chairs, and call it a dining room suite. Americans were becoming more sophisticated and with dis-

---

2 Robert Marks, "Hickory Area Mart Opens First", High Point Enterprise, October 17, 1965, p. 2.
3 Robert Marks, "Hickory Area Mart Opens First", High Point Enterprise, October 17, 1965, p. 2.
4 Robert Marks, "Hickory Area Mart Opens First", High Point Enterprise, October 17, 1965, p. 2.
5 Robert Marks, "Hickory Area Mart Opens First", High Point Enterprise, October 17, 1965, p. 2.

posable income, earmarked for the furnishing of their home, they wanted to see more. So did the store owners through which they would buy.

The frenzy of sales had been good for North Carolina, particularly in two regions. Right around the same time in the last decade of the 19th century, furniture production began to take hold in and around High Point, in southern Guildford County and in northwest North Carolina. Morganton, Lenoir and Hickory (in that order) all started making items crafted from nearby wood. They grew into a powerful triumvirate, rivaled only by the High Point companies as the center of Southern furniture making. Though there were other companies in other places, like southern Virginia, High Point and Hickory became the place retail furniture store owners came to see what was new and exciting in furniture. Groupings they could buy at wholesale and sell at retail all over the country would distribute the products of those factories nationwide and serve as an economic driver for the two cities.

By the 1950s it became apparent that these store owners needed to see the styles from a lot of different companies quickly and compactly. The furniture showroom was born. While some furniture makers tried to lure buyers to their factories where they had set up showrooms of their own product, the drive from one place to another became tremendously unwieldy and a solution was needed. The city of Hickory, sensing an opportunity set up the first multi-manufacturer showroom in 1953. It was followed in 1960 when Julius Mull started Hickory Furniture Mart on the southeastern outskirts (at the time) of the city in 1960.

In 1963 when Graham Leroy Lail, Jr. returned from service as a Naval officer, he sensed the growth of the showroom concept for buyers too. His father-in-law took 6,000 square feet of basement space under his restaurant and turned it into the Hickory Furniture Mart. The showroom was always secondary to not only the restaurant but also the motel upstairs. Mr. Mull asked his son-in-law if he could take over management of the Mart. Lail did. In fact, he quickly took the bull by the horns with plans to expand HFM and attract a variety of manufacturers who would in turn attract more buyers.

"At the Hickory Furniture Mart, Graham (Leroy) Lail reports long-range planning is under way for further expansion of this building. 'We have nothing definite yet, but we are thinking along those lines,' Lail says."[6] With Hickory Furniture Mart as his primary focus, he began envisioning the possibilities of a grander facility, able to entice a greater percentage of both furniture companies and furniture buyers. His timing was perfect.

Within a quick few years, Hickory was crawling with furniture buyers, invading every spring and fall to see the new lines and place orders. By 1967 reports read, "more than 4,000 furniture dealers are expected in Hickory today for the opening of the fall Furniture Market. There will be 38 exhibits at the Home Furnishings Mart, 52 at the Hickory Furniture Mart, and 10 other showrooms in Hickory operated by the manufacturers themselves will be open."[7] It hadn't taken Leroy Lail long to push the basement showroom into the largest and most accommodating stop for seeing the most sweeping variety of furniture west of High Point.

Business was well beyond good, it was great. Lail, keeping tabs on

---
6   Robert Marks, "For Furniture Marketing, New Air of Cooperation," High Point Enterprise, April 22, 1966, p. 18.
7   "Hickory Expects 4,000 Furniture Men Today", Charlotte Observer, October 20, 1967, p. 3.

how many visitors were coming to his Hickory Furniture Mart, became the person to ask about the pulse of the market. For the spring market of 1968 he was in high spirits. "G. Leroy Lail, manager of the Hickory Furniture Mart, says attendance at his showroom is more than 30 percent higher than at the 1967 spring market. He adds that all indications are that buying volume is in tune with the increase in traffic."[8]

The uptick came even with a turbulent time in America. The market that year welcomed buyers from all fifty states, "but there are reports some buyers from Baltimore and other metropolitan areas hit hard by recent racial disturbances did not show up for this market."[9] 1968 brought more than its share of violent and chaotic events with the assassinations of both Dr. Martin Luther King, Jr. and Robert Kennedy (who was running for president at the time) in the first half of the year. Later, the Democratic National Convention in Chicago would be marked by protests, met with televised police beatings.

By this point, furniture buyers had settled into a routine and the industry had a name for it. Wanting to see all that every company had to offer, retailers swarmed to Hickory and High Point, selling out motel space, crowding restaurants and spending quite a bit of money in the process. They got out their maps and planned a caravan of sorts to travel to each of the destinations that sported showrooms. Manufacturers called it the "Furniture Figure Eight." High Point, Thomasville and Winston-Salem provided a loop for touring in the east, Morganton, Lenoir and Hickory did the same in the west, with the city of Statesville (who had a few

---

8   "Optimism Still High at Furniture Market", News & Observer (Raleigh), April 23, 1968, p. 3.
9   "Optimism Still High at Furniture Market", News & Observer (Raleigh), April 23, 1968, p. 3.

showrooms) the central, connecting city. On the map, it looked like an eight on its side.

The election of Richard Nixon marked the end of the overt turmoil that gripped the nation in 1968 and quickly business got back to its expansive self. New ideas were quickly on the horizon. The January 1969 market opening for "Western Figure Eight Furniture Market" included 14 manufacturers including Hickory Furniture Mart.[10] If April and October were good, Leroy Lail thought a market in between markets might also catch on. He continued to look for a competitive advantage. The idea of showing furniture for wholesale buyers was catching on. Los Angeles, California had begun a spring market by 1969, seeking to repeat North Carolina's success. While it was a reminder of the dog-eat-dog world of commerce, few back on the western end of the furniture figure eight paid much attention. "Few southern or eastern manufacturers would show at the Los Angeles market, said Graham (Leroy) Lail, Managing Director of Hickory Furniture Mart."[11] He had his hands full with the thousands who were stopping at his ever-growing Hickory Furniture Mart to see the lines of furniture within.

At the same time, Leroy Lail was growing Hickory Furniture Mart, his own family was growing too. Son Scott Lail recalled that the "Furniture Mart looms large in my mind, mainly because I was born in 1963 and dad, I think, came to work here shortly thereafter." As he grew up, he remembered coming to his father's office, at a corner just inside the North entrance. "It had a sign that said 'General Manager' on it and I remember that being his first office. When I was young, with the Mart

---
10   "Western Furniture Market", High Point Enterprise, January 19, 1969, p. 2.
11   Robert Marks, "No Still Made Over LA Markets", High Point Enterprise, March 19, 1969, p. 23.

only being open twice a year, there were a lot of times where it was dark and there was not a lot of people in there at all."

For a young Scott Lail, the empty showroom was something of "a playground for a kid to run around and run up the steps and run down the hallway." On one occasion, it also became a trap. "I remember the railings and we still have the same railings. I got my head stuck in between the rails. When I was young my head was small. I think dad had to come rescue me from that." Since the Mart was a family business, the younger Lail was soon introduced to a job maintain the Mart between markets. "One of my first jobs at the Furniture Mart was vacuuming the carpet. Hickory Furniture Mart, if I recall correctly, had green shag carpet pretty much everywhere, and one of my jobs was to vacuum the carpet and they liked for me to vacuum the carpet one way this way and another that way to create a pattern." It was not the last time his responsibilities included keeping the complex clean for the next Furniture Market.

His first paid job came as a twelve-year-old. Anxious to buy a ten-speed bike at a local Hickory store, he worked all summer "picking up cigarette butts and pulling weeds in front of Mull's Restaurant and all around Hickory Furniture Mart." Every Wednesday "from 7:30 (am) until about 2:00 (pm)" he clocked in and worked the asphalt until it was clear of all debris. "When I was a kid that was the longest day." For him, time seemed to drag as he waited to join his younger brother and sister when his mother Lynn brought them to the pool. Looking back on it, he recalled the bike cost just over a hundred dollars and for working every Wednesday to get it, he said, "I don't think I was paid all that well."[12]

Furniture buyers came from everywhere, even California. But as

---
[12] Interview with Scott Lail, Hickory Furniture Mart, September 2, 2020.

a man who grew up near Hickory (in the St. Stephens community northeast of town), Leroy Lail remained cognizant of the fact that Hickory Furniture Mart was a part of the local community. His Mart attracted huge crowds twice a year, but in order to make use of his facility he welcomed local organizations to come and also enjoy the atmosphere he created for the out-of-town set. "A fashion show, 'Fashions For A Day In May,' will be held May 8 at 8 p.m. at the Hickory Furniture Mart, sponsored by the Conover Junior Woman's Club. Fashions from Spainhours will be modeled, and Gloria Baker will be commentator. Proceeds will go toward a scholarship,"[13] read one notice.

Boarding up Hickory Furniture Mart after each market was not in Leroy Lail's plans. It didn't make good sense for the building, even though he used the intervals to expand, nor did it make sense for recognition of the Mart. By the late 60s, Lail recognized that he was good at two things, building and promoting. He kept architects busy with the first and himself busy with the second, asking himself how he could promote Hickory Furniture Mart to Hickory and the world. Planning for and cleaning up after each market might be enough for some, but not him. He embarked upon a variety of uses for Hickory Furniture Mart that did not always involve furniture.

To accommodate Leroy Lail's vision for expansion, he found opportunities to solve issues that concerned his manufacturing tenants. Some complained that the entryway disadvantaged them. The Mart contained two floors, only 20,000 square-feet. Those on the bottom floor said people entering the building started upstairs. Lail decided to solve the problem by changing the approach to each level. He installed "bi-parted"

---

13   "May Fashions to Be Shown", Charlotte Observer, April 24, 1969, p. 2C.

stairs. One flight of steps took buyers up, right beside a flight that took them down. Now the choice solely belonged to the person in the building.[14]

The Hickory Furniture Mart building featured a number of innovations like the bi-parted stairs that facilitated dealers as they strolled through. One day in the mid-1960s, Leroy Lail was thinking about expanding the facility when an idea came. He was looking out the back and in his head, a 'mall type' environment came to him. "I'd never even seen a mall before," said Lail about the concept. "In those days, no one had," he added. Stepping off the space he believed would be necessary for the addition he began to plan another (lower) floor for the Mart, with an interior courtyard. During his next lull between markets, he made his first addition to the south end, creating a way for customers to survey the array. Since then, most of the Mart has sprinklers.[15]

As it turned out, one innovation led to the next. The Mart needed water for sprinkler systems in order to build larger rooms within it. Twelve thousand square feet was the limit for a room without dedicated fire protection. The building code that specified such restriction hampered the growth that Leroy Lail envisioned. "What I had to do early on was put in a series of fire walls," he said. He joked that there are a lot of people at the Mart who don't know why there are these thick walls with fire doors but they were part of the early growth.[16]

In the early days, the Mart relied on the same system used by the Mull's Motel and Restaurant complex, a well and sewer treatment plant that Lail himself checked on a daily basis. But the Mart was grow-

---

14 Interview with Leroy Lail, September 29, 2020, Conover, NC.
15 Interview with Leroy Lail, September 29, 2020, Conover, NC.
16 Interview with Leroy Lail, September 29, 2020, Conover, NC.

ing between every market. So Leroy Lail embarked on getting water and sewer lines to make future enlargement feasible. When the property came under the jurisdiction of the City of Hickory (not yet within city limits but in their planning zone), he paid for the line to be extended a half mile to reach the Mart. In doing so, Lail paved the way for development of a stretch of Highway 70 that has become the region's most popular, home to Valley Hills Mall, numerous shopping centers and most famously, HFM.[17]

With water, came sprinkler systems that allowed the Mart to construct larger rooms. As Leroy Lail has always said, "you need four things to make business happen: water, sewer, roads and people." He had taken care of the first two out of his own pocket. Highway 70 ran right past the Mart and was expanding from a two-lane road to a five-lane thoroughfare. The popularity of the Mart took care of the people. With each of these Lail said, "I just really enjoyed in each case, solving the problem. It was an opportunity to grow and improve."[18]

The early additions came when the Mart was still in the county. Lail remembered, "I would build the building, then just go down to the county and ask them for a building permit and I would get it." But once the inspector for the city came down and required a permit before construction, "I had to hire an architect. His name was Bill Reinhardt and I worked with him for the rest of his life." After that, Lail and Reinhardt worked together on all of Lail's other properties.[19]

"Once I got into it, I was planning for the next addition," said Leroy Lail about his expansions of Hickory Furniture Mart. On one trip to

---

17   Interview with Leroy Lail, September 29, 2020, Conover, NC.
18   Interview with Leroy Lail, September 29, 2020, Conover, NC.
19   Interview with Leroy Lail, September 29, 2020, Conover, NC.

Atlanta, he saw a glass elevator and decided he needed one for his growing Mart. He petitioned the state to build one. His thinking was that an elevator with glass would give riders a better view of all the floors of the Mart. On his first try, the state turned him down. Then when he saw a partially glassed exterior elevator at Winston-Salem's newly constructed parking garage, he renewed his request, this time succeeding. Its construction in 1974 gave the glass elevator at Hickory Furniture Mart the first interior one of its kind in North Carolina. The elevator was perhaps the most visual example of Leroy Lail's mantra. "I love to build and I love to promote." After its construction, he promoted the addition of the glass elevator and numerous expansions with a visit by the lieutenant governor to bring attention to the innovative and ever-enlarging complex. As Lail concedes, "I was constantly trying to do things differently."[20]

With the 1970s came diverse reasons to drive to the Mart. Lail booked a variety of events. In the years before Hickory formally created its own convention center (which he spearheaded and built), Hickory Furniture Mart welcomed numerous and far ranging gatherings. In 1971, the Catawba Valley Chapter of the American Institute of Banking held a meeting at HFM with J. Kenneth Clark, VP of NCNB speaking on "Talking is Easy, Communicating Is Not."[21] Hickory Motor Speedway, located just down the road from the Mart, started holding its annual Awards Banquet at the Hickory Furniture Mart. One year NASCAR driver Benny Parsons served as guest speaker. The event was open to the public.[22]

Even industries that competed with furniture for workers and

---

20   Interview with Leroy Lail, September 29, 2020, Conover, NC.
21   "Talk Set By Clark", Statesville Record and Landmark, March 22, 1971, p. 8.
22   "Awards Banquet Tonight", Statesville Record and Landmark, February 3, 1973, p. 14' "Circling the Circuit", Charlotte Observer, January 20, 1974, p. 32.

notoriety in the area were invited to hold sessions. The Catawba Valley Hosiery Exposition moved its Hickory Hosiery Show to the Hickory Furniture Mart from the Hickory Foundation Center, becoming the area's premier location for activities. According to the High Point Enterprise, always a keen observer of what furniture-related facilities were doing, it reported, "the Furniture Mart proposes to make its facilities available, provide registration staff, supply cleaning services, enlarge doors to allow movement in of heavy machinery and (also reserved) a block of rooms in the motel complex to selected participants at the exposition. It is figured to use some 10,000 feet, with additional space to be available as needed. It begins to appear furniture and hosiery do mix and a new day is nearing for the Hickory Hosiery Show."[23]

Conventions large and small filled the calendar. Just in front of the 1974's fall market came stitchers of all levels when the "Needlework Fair" came to HFM September 19-21, 1974.[24] Each year the 'needle-point-ers' expanded their offerings. "Workshops, demonstration booths and a needlework competition will highlight the Western Piedmont Symphony Guild's Needlework Fair Friday and Saturday, February 27 and 28, at the Hickory Furniture Mart."[25] The following year they began to brand their event as an annual and ongoing event, naming it "Needlework Fair '77."[26] Be they race fans or knitters, a wide array of folks were coming that might never have been within the walls of HFM if not for its expanding mission.

---

23   High Point Enterprise, February 15, 1973, p. 2.
24   Robert Marks, High Point Enterprise, August 18, 1974, p. 33.
25   "Symphony Guild's Needlework Fair Offers Prizes", Charlotte Observer (CO), February 8, 1976, p. 10E.
26   "Needlework Fair Set in Hickory:, February 22, 1977, Statesville Record & Landmark, February 22, 1977, p. 7.

But at the heart of attractions of Hickory Furniture Mart was furniture. Many events supported the idea of HFM as a central location for home furnishings. So it was not out of the realm of logic that an "Antique Show and Sale at the Hickory Furniture Mart brought more attendees in March of 1973."[27] A number of events were connected even more directly. Sensing the area's interest in how the market went, what styles were popular and how they might get in on some of it, Leroy Lail decided it was time to give them a peek. For years, local folks had knocked on the doors of the Mart, seeking to look and perhaps buy (hopefully at wholesale prices). He or one of his employees had to give them the bad news that the Furniture Market did not offer such entry to consumers. But in 1972 he had an idea. Why not create an open house "to give the public a sneak preview of new furniture styles." As a responsible member of the Hickory community he staged a showing on the heels of the market, "sponsored by the Hickory Jaycettes and the Hickory Chamber of Commerce. Proceeds go to the Cystic Fibrosis chapter in Hickory. Sunday, October 29, 1972, 1-5pm." The event was so successful it ran for concurrent years.[28]

Another way Leroy Lail invited the community to participate in the twice yearly markets was to help his presenters make use of the extraordinary level of talent in the area. "Brenda Rose, (was) selected by the Masland Duraleather Company to participate in the Duran Cover Girl Program at the Hickory Furniture Mart. A junior from Lenoir-Rhyne College, Rose presented "the company's advertising program to furniture buyers." Masland made "vinyl upholstery for furniture manufacturers."

---

27   Charlotte News (classified), March 1, 1973, p. 30.
28   "Open House Set at Furniture Marts", Asheville Citizen-Times, September 27, 1972, p. 25; "Open House Ends Fall Show", Statesville Record & Landmark, October 31, 1972, p. 13; "Open House is Planned by Jaycettes" Statesville Record & Landmark, October 6, 1973, p. 5.

She became one of four finalists for a $1000 scholarship, awarded by Masland.[29] Deborah Mesenheimer of Rockwell was "named 1973 Masland Cover Girl for the Hickory Furniture Market," the following year.[30]

Builders large and small displayed at Hickory Furniture Mart. One of the quirkier examples was a Connecticut couple who made drum tables. Mary Ann Cameron called her tables "drums with a historical beat." She researched the design and use of Revolutionary War field drums as a model for a furniture accessory, made with the assistance of her husband Russell. She not only sold the tables "at the company's booth in the Hickory Furniture Mart," she also gave buyers a history lesson in the value of drums for the armies of American independence. The motif included the use of American eagles and a "moonface" that the Camerons referred to as "Humpty-Dumpty," used in the battle of Guilford Court House, now part of Greensboro. The drum table fit well with the Early American designs, produced by all the major manufacturers of the period. "Most of the Cameron drum tables come in lamp and cocktail table sizes. One cocktail table's top is a lift-out lid so that it doubles as a bin for children's toys."[31]

Hickory Furniture Mart had gotten crowded. To alleviate the situation, Leroy Lail employed architects again to create more space. With a bit of history as background, the High Point Enterprise reported that "the Hickory Furniture Mart has added 35,000 square feet of space to its building. Opened in 1960 with 6,000 square feet of space for furniture exhib-

---

29 "Local Girl Has Eventful Experiences at College", The Robesonian, January 21, 1973, p. 10.
30 "Rockwell Student Named Cover Girl", Statesville Record & Landmark, April 24, 1973, p. 6.
31 Barbara Ingold, "Brum Tables Have a Historical Beat", Charlotte Observer, December 6, 1969, p. 8.

itors, the Hickory Furniture Mart now has 335,000 square feet of space being used by 80 exhibitors."[32] By the fall market of 1975 that renovation was complete and the expansion had been even bigger than planned. "Construction on a 42,000-square-foot addition to Hickory Furniture Mart will be complete in time for a grand opening on October 23, according to G. Leroy Lail, Mart Manager. The four-story addition is completely rented, and a new 150-car lot is being constructed to handle the increased traffic to be generated by the new exhibitors, Lail said."[33]

The buzz of what was new and what still held sway was always a topic of conversation as each market approached. HFM, and its displayers made sure to be a leading indicator of where the furniture industry was going in design. One observation read, "the fully upholstered look is still around. In Lenoir, Bernhardt went so far as to upholster bun feet on some pieces. And at the Hickory Furniture Mart, ICD Furniture of Ontario, Canada, showed a soft line of two-drawer chests, upholstered to double as benches.[34]

By the fall market of 1975, sales were better than ever, with "according to every major indicator, the largest home furnishings show in the history of the industry." The Furniture Manufacturers Marketing Assn. of the South expanded to a ninth day "so that buyers might have additional time to travel to market." The Hickory Furniture Mart added another 85,000 square feet of space.[35]

The 1975 markets served as a watershed for HFM. With each sur-

---

32   Robert Marks, "Finest Market Seen", High Point Enterprise, April 13, 1975, p. 1.
33   "Mart Addition", High Point Enterprise, September 30, 1975, p. 5.
34   Ellen Scarborough, "Upholstered Furniture Comes on Soft", Charlotte Observer (CO), April 22, 1975, p. 6.
35   Robert Marks, "Biggest Show Ever Slated for Market", High Point Enterprise, October 19, 1975, p. 2.

passing the previous for sales and attendance, enlargement was needed. The news attracted the inevitable attention of the press.

"Hickory Furniture Mart has announced plans for a 300,000-square-foot addition in the burgeoning Southern Furniture Market. The furniture exhibition building is located on Highway 64-70 east of Hickory, in the Mull's Motel and Mull's Restaurant complex. The present Mart building is a four-story structure containing 300,000 square feet."

"Announcement of the expansion came from G. Leroy Lail, president, who said, 'The building we have on the planning board is not only visually exciting, it is a model of up-to-the-minute energy-saving features that should be benchmarks in area construction.'"

"With the planned twelve-story addition, the Hickory Furniture Mart will become the largest non-production building in Catawba County. Architect William P. Reinhardt of Newton said, 'This has been one of the most challenging and one of the most rewarding buildings our firm has ever designed. Of course, the fact that the present Hickory Furniture Mart was designed with this addition in mind is a plus. And, our prior experience with the problems of the Mart construction have helped us to perfect our present design.'"

"Interior design of the new building will be by Jim McDonald Associates of Los Angeles, California. McDonald, a specialist in large space concepts, has worked extensively in the United States and Canada. He holds a number of design awards.

"Lail said, 'After studying many existing Mart buildings throughout the country, as well as the latest techniques in construction and space utilization, we set three basic criteria. First, we wanted energy consumption kept at a minimum. Second, we wanted the building to be the essence of efficiency for visiting and shopping. And, third, we wanted extreme flexibility to meet tenant needs.'

"The building will have a mall interior courtyard designed to take advantage of natural energy sources. A body of water will supply a focal point from a decorative standpoint, while the water is used to help cool the building. Lail said that solar radiation from overhead roof panels would conduct heat to the interior of the building, where a system of baffles and sliding overhead panels would be used.

The addition will be constructed at the west end of the present Hickory Furniture Mart, on part of a 35-acre tract owned by the complex."[36]

When construction was complete, the news media was back to report on the accomplishment. "A three story addition to Hickory Furniture Mart will be ready for occupancy in time for the Fall Southern Furniture Market this week. The new section is located on the south side of the Mart and, as an extension to the galleria, will provide space for more exhibitors.[37]

Before the arrival of the next Furniture Market came news that Hickory Furniture Mart's founder, "Julius P. Mull, 85, retired owner and

---
36   "Hickory Market Announces Plan For Expansion", High Point Enterprise, April 22, 1976, p. 17.
37   "Hickory Mart", High Point Enterprise, October 13, 1976, p. 2.

founder of Mulls Motel-Restaurant and Hickory Furniture Mart, and owner of Catawba Marble and Granite Co., died Wednesday."[38] The news did not do justice to the fact that Mr. Mull had begun the Mart well before furniture showrooms had become big business and his vision to select his son-in-law to propel HFM to new heights had been a key event in Hickory's development to make the city synonymous with the Furniture Market.

Building project followed building project throughout the seventies. After the year following the great expansion, came yet another. Each time the design was intended to outdo the previous. "Hickory Furniture Mart plans a 4-story, 30,000-square-feet addition to be completed in time for the October Furniture Show. Work already is underway on a 10-story tower, constructed around an atrium and featuring exterior glass elevators," read one account.[39] Though the ten-story tower was sacrificed for the overall aesthetic of the complex, the creation was still big, bold and ready to welcome a larger than ever Southern Furniture Market.

The spring of 1978 saw "more than 35,000 furniture buyers, makers, suppliers and exhibitors" arriving to begin their perusal of manufacturers' best (products). Development at HFM only strengthened Hickory's value to the overall 'furniture-figure-eight' but differences remained. As it had since its beginning the official start date of the market remained a point of contention between the two circles forming the 'eight.' "Although the spring market officially opens its nine-day run Thursday, the major exhibition buildings in Hickory opened their doors Tuesday," reported Raleigh's News and Observer.

The conflict paled in the light of the business getting ready to be

---

38   Charlotte Observer (CO), March 4, 1977, p. 10.
39   "F.Y.I. Today", Charlotte Observer, April 29, 1977, p. 4C.

made by the influx of furniture retailers. As the Raleigh paper continued, "the market, a top attraction in the nation's furniture industry, is expected to draw visitors from all 50 states and 40 foreign nations. Officials estimate that 85 percent of the nation's retail furniture buying power will be represented at the market." The numbers showed that the eyes of the furniture world were on Hickory and High Point and a small matter like a day or two in letting buyers in on the lines ready for purchase were trivial, but still reported. "There has been a dispute among market officials in the Hickory-Morganton-Lenoir area in the western part of the state and High Point to the east for several years over the opening of exhibitions each spring." The notice then got specific about where the early openings were occurring. "The Furniture Factories Marketing Association of the South (FFMAS), which sets the rules for the market and serves as its official host, has unsuccessfully tried to decide on a date for all the exhibitions to open. However, HIckory's three major buildings are still opening their showrooms two days earlier than those in the High Point area."

The disagreement drew a quote from the head of FFMAS. "We would still like to see the situation correct itself, but will not continue to wage a major campaign," said Richard Barentine, Executive Director of the association. A number of companies that offered their own showrooms had nominally gotten in line with the official start date, but not three important showrooms in Hickory. "He pointed out that the three exhibition buildings - Hickory Furniture Mart, Hickory Home Furnishings Mart and Hickory Merchandise Mart - are only associate members and therefore not subject to the organization's rules. Those who favor the early opening say many of the major manufacturers have 'pre-market' in their private showrooms to exhibit their products."⁴⁰ With so much business at stake FFMAS accepted the start date issue and watched the business roll in.

The issue had been around as long as the Hickory showrooms themselves. After the establishment of Hickory Furniture Mart in 1960, the group that sponsored a similar showroom in the basement of the Hickory Foundation Center decided to build their own structure in 1964. The imposing and sprawling complex along Highway 321 in northwest Hickory always lagged behind HFM in vendors and space. Likewise, the creation of the Hickory Merchandise Mart was created when a group of furniture manufacturers that had previously displayed at HFM believed they could compete successfully, seeing the amount of business being done. But still HFM led the way among Hickory showrooms in importance, space and expansion.

For furniture manufacturing companies, the real estate at HFM was so crucial for those all-important markets that one company decided to make sure it would be represented well beyond the two months when buyers came to town. Trend Line Furniture Corporation of Hickory announced its intention to lease space from HFM with the intention to locate its corporate headquarters there. In a "12,000-square-foot building being constructed adjacent to the existing complex," Trend Line also planned to relocate its showrooms in the Mart. Its upholstery plants were located within quick proximity to the Mart, in Conover and Lincolnton with its trucking terminal in Conover.⁴¹

Soon after Montclair Furniture Co. did the same thing. Its plants

---

40   "Furniture Market Opening", News & Observer (Raleigh), April 12, 1978, p. 10.
41   "F.Y.I. Today", CO, September 16, 1978, p. 8.

were even closer to HFM (Conover and Claremont in Catawba County), the manufacturer that employed about 400 workers decided to take their old offices and convert them into "additional manufacturing room."[42]

The move of both companies put them into the thick of activity each April and October and gave them a better vantage point from which to plan their next market. As each six months passed and a new market arrived, HFM helped to welcome buyers with a touch of western North Carolina life. In 1979 the announcement was made that "the traditional apple cider will again be offered to buyers and sellers at Hickory Furniture Mart."[43] In addition, "hot dogs served on a brick patio, a glass-walled elevator and classic cars exhibited outside," making visitors feel at home and ready to buy.

Like 1968, 1979 presented some obstacles borne out of the times folks faced. But this time it seemed Leroy Lail could turn a negative into a positive. That spring Americans faced a gas shortage brought on by oil producing nations in the Middle East as retaliation for the actions of then President Jimmy Carter and his humanitarian efforts to allow entry to the deposed leader of Iran. For the first time gas spiked in price to over a dollar a gallon. "'With people traveling less because of the gas shortage… people will be wanting to buy things to make home a better place to be,' says Leroy Lail, president of Hickory Furniture Mart, one of Hickory's three permanent display centers." Lail's judgement of the situation proved to be prescient. H.W. "Buddy" Sherrill, president of Sherrill Upholstery Company and a displayer at HFM agreed. "Home buying is expected to remain a favorite hedge against inflation, despite soaring interest rates…

---
42   "F.Y.I. Today", CO, October 4, 1978, p. 4C.
43   Bruce Henderson, "Furniture Fever Epidemic Grips Catawba County", CO, April 18, 1979, p. 16.

And homes do have to be furnished," he said."[44] The Southern Furniture Market remained strong that year.

The atmosphere in Hickory was one of putting its best foot forward. However, visitors were not always pleased with the amenities outside HFM and balked at what Greater Hickory had to offer. "I wished there were better restaurants," was the critique of Jan Moody, a New York executive. She expected accommodations more like those from where she came than the small North Carolina town to which she came to buy furniture. She added, "I cannot understand why this area, that has grown so tremendously in the last five years, cannot have an airport where planes (from larger airlines) can land."[45]

By 1979, the spring and fall markets were not enough. In High Point, winter and summer markets, smaller in scope were attracting a different kind of dealer. Though he had tried it once before at the beginning of the decade with tepid success, it did not stop the man who often said, "if at first you don't succeed, try, try again. "'We felt like it was reasonable for us to have a market in January and July,' as High Point has, said Leroy Lail of Hickory Furniture Mart and Hickory Merchandise Mart. 'A lot of small retailers prefer it.'"[46]

Early reports indicated that the time for the idea had come. The four-day market expected "as many as 4,800 retail buyers from 2,100 stores in North Carolina, South Carolina, Virginia, West Virginia, Maryland, Kentucky, Tennessee, and Washington, D.C." to come to both Hickory and High Point. For Hickory's part, Leroy Lail saw opportunity in

---

44   LaFleur Paysour, "3,000 Buyers Flock to Furniture Market", CO, October 16, 1979, p. B2
45   Bruce Henderson, "Furniture Mart Bubbles", CO, April 25, 1979, p. C1.
46   Bruce Henderson, "Regional Furniture Market Coming to Hickory", CO, November 20, 1979, p. B1.

the off season market saying that "much of the Hickory promotion would feature seminars stressing professionalism at the furniture retail level, which he said would be increasingly important as the industry caters to more affluent and sophisticated customers." The other advantage to what he called "a less chaotic market" was a place where "we could spend a little more time with them (customers)." In Hickory alone, "Lail estimated that as many as 700 retailers would visit Hickory next week, compared with the 10,000 to 12,000 who usually attend the larger markets."[47]

Markets of various sizes four times a year kept everyone busier but also raised the level of business to new heights. Still there was time for other considerations at HFM. In 1980, Mart officials played host to "the N.C. Department of Commerce, the Catawba County Chamber of Commerce and Industrial Development Commission and the Carolinas-Virginia Purchasing Management Association" who held a buyer-supplier conference at the Mart.[48]

Everyone from the City of Hickory to the Mart itself were always conscious that in order to secure a profitable market, buyers needed to be treated well while they were there. HFM in 1980 decided that what visitors wanted was access to more sporting activities. So when the Mart prepared for the coming market they also added amenities."The Furniture Mart offers services ranging from motel space and dining to a health center and tennis courts. This year, a racquetball court has been added. The two-story court has one side made entirely of glass, enabling viewers to sit on the patio and not miss any of the action."[49]

Buyers also wanted to party, not always an easy endeavor in

---
47   "Hickory to Join winter market", News & Observer (Raleigh), January 5, 1980, p. 24.
48   "F.Y.I. Today", CO, February 15, 1980, p. B6.
49   Asheville Citizen-Times, March 16, 1980, p. 4D.

Hickory. "To the clink of uplifted cocktail glasses and the lively notes of dance bands, market hosts will do their best to entertain clients in a city where commercial nightlife is scarce. Hickory Furniture Mart employee in charge of staging the "dance halls," Lois Snyder said, "it makes good sense." She elaborated that doing so only aided business. "You entertain them, you feed them - and you can still talk business over a drink." Among the fun, ostensibly to celebrate Hickory Furniture Mart's 20th anniversary, were several "manufacturer-sponsored cocktail parties." If that wasn't enough "Mart president Leroy Lail plans to seal a furniture-oriented time capsule Sunday to be opened in the year 2000." The atmosphere was lively with "mixers, wine and cheese and cocktail parties to the tunes of such groups as the Ruby Reds Warehouse Band jazz group. A Saturday dining-and-dancing 'Las Vegas Night' will be staged at Hickory Furniture Mart."[50]

In between the lavish parties entertaining guests at each Furniture Market, Leroy Lail and his staff continued to seek events to open the doors of the now huge complex. Their work drew such unexpected prospects at the "Allied Stores Marketing Corp., a subsidiary of New York-based Allied Stores Corp.," which hosted "a seminar at the Hickory Furniture Mart's Meeting Center."[51] Additionally, HFM served as an impressive backdrop when such luminaries as North Carolina's Lt. Governor came to town. One account read, "Lt. Gov. Jimmy Green was at Hickory Furniture Mart Wednesday to present $450 in furniture technology scholarships for Catawba Valley Technical College."[52]

---

50   Bruce Henderson, "Spring Market Kicks Off", CO, April 15, 1980, p. B1.
51   "Business and Farm", News & Observer (Raleigh), October 7, 1980, p. 20.
52   Bruce Henderson, "Thousands of Buyers Jam Area For Southern Furniture Market", CO, October 23, 1980, p. D1.

The idea of staged events went over well. HFM let the local community get in on the revelry, with "A 'Monte Carlo Night' tonight, sponsored by the Catawba County Arts Council." The event showcased "local artists during the fall Southern Furniture Market." The buffet dinner at 7:30 (pm)" was followed by songs from Julia Rush Harrell, a popular favorite in Hickory."[53]

The most bizarre occurrence within the walls was a wedding that took place during the fall 1981 market. Jackie Groban met Karen Mims at Montclair Furniture in Claremont, where he was a sales director and she an assistant to the firm's vice-president. Since it was a "match made at market" the couple chose to conduct the ceremony for 150 guests in the "far corner" so that attendees had to "pick their way through Montclair's fall lineup." The bride giggled when she admitted that "everybody's kidding Jackie about not carrying his order pad up to the altar." Always a salesman and something of a stand-up comic too, Groban saw his nuptials as a chance to do double duty. Besides bringing old friends together for the joyous occasion, he also quipped, "I got 'em in the door, didn't I?"[54]

Every fall and spring, Furniture Market meant a lot of work for everyone, and that included the Lail family. Unbeknownst to many who were involved in the manual labor of hauling furniture to showroom floors, Leroy Lail's oldest son Scott was one of the workers. He would one day return to the family business as a leader in the financial side of operations but in the early 1980s he was lugging sofas around, calling it "quite a lot of work." Recalling the activity, "I worked pretty much, every market that they had helping move the furniture in." He added, "the furniture

---

53   "Catawba Arts Council", CO, October 25, 1980, p. 3C.
54   Bruce Henderson, "Couple Celebrate Match Made at Market", CO, October 21, 1981, p. C2.

would come in on the trucks and there would be a crew of us, usually about four or five younger guys and we would be in charge of getting it off the truck, unboxing the furniture and then getting it into the showrooms."⁵⁵

Scott Lail's connection to both the owners and workers turned out to be awkward on occasion. Admitting that often, folks with which he was shoulder to shoulder did not realize that connection, he called it "a little bit of a surprise" when they found out. "I remember sometimes people didn't know that I was Leroy's son. I didn't let on I was Leroy's son either, said Lail. "Then when they did find out, it was almost like, I wouldn't call it fear, but it was almost like, 'Oh, did I say anything that I shouldn't?'" According to Lail, the admission was always greeted with "surprise when I was revealed to be the oldest son of Leroy."⁵⁶

As times were changing in America, so too was the wholesale Furniture Market. By 1982, observers noted. "some furniture companies appear to be belt-tightening on their showroom renovations for April's Southern Furniture Market." The changes were felt at HFM. "One of Hickory's major showrooms, the Hickory Furniture Mart, figures the 90 furniture makers who exhibit in the building are spending about $250,000 on renovations for the April 15-23 market. 'That's flat or down slightly from last year,' John Schenk, Vice President, says."

Manufacturers were just not spending a lot of money to showcase their newest designs. "Exhibits are overhauled before each show, held in April and October. Companies build elaborate bedroom, living room and dining room settings for showing off their new and most popular

---

55 Interview with Scott Lail, Hickory Furniture Mart, September 2, 2020.
56 Interview with Scot Lail, Hickory Furniture Mart, September 2, 2020.

lines," relayed the reporting on the downsizing. Some of it was attributable to the economic downturn which had been in progress since the gas shortage. "They're not doing the drastic changes to showroom space like tearing out walls. Instead," Shenck noted "many are working more within existing layouts and concentrating on details and window dressing."[57] Some just saw it as a momentary pause but others sensed substantive change was in the air.

Hickory had always been the junior partner to High Point in the semi-annual market. Though trucks from furniture factories in Lenoir and Hickory proclaimed the western half of the "figure eight" to be the "Furniture Capital of the World," officials in High Point kept up the pressure of trying to force Hickory showrooms to adhere to the designated start date for each market. They failed. In 1982, Hickory locales opened their doors two days before High Point. It had become what one reporter called, "a tradition." That year "about 1,300 manufacturers participate(d)" in the market, over a stretch of 150 miles that separated the two halves. And while High Point wrung it hands over the start date saying that some "manufacturers have said they worry that separate starting days could upset the balance of showroom traffic by focusing more attention on Hickory at the market's opening and less at its closing," it didn't stop western showrooms from opening early. "G. Leroy Lail, President of the Hickory Furniture Mart, a major Hickory showroom, said in a prepared statement that the new policy "is intended to create a more pleasant market experience for furniture dealers. It will add additional structure to the marketplace, eliminate confusion and create a better atmosphere for furniture

---

57   "Austere Settings A Trend Among Furniture Exhibitors", CO, March 22, 1982, p. 6D.

dealers in which to visit and shop."[58]

The controversy did not affect buyers who were eager to shop and appreciated the added consideration. Since they were the drivers of a productive market, it paid to keep them happy. The fall market opened with a bang. "The Southern Furniture Market opened in Hickory on an upbeat note Tuesday as furniture retailers and manufacturers welcomed falling interest rates and prospects for an upturn in the economy." There remained some tensions as to the timing of the market in the volatile economic cycle as "buyers and sellers said the encouraging economic news comes too late to increase orders in the 10-day fall market.[59]

Leroy Lail chose to remain optimistic, saying "I see a lot of smiles, a lot of good feeling." The fullness of the parking lot was one indicator that things were going well. Still, everyone was edgy. Interest rates were going down and the stock market was going up, good signs for an improved economy which generally saw furniture as the first commodity to get cancelled by consumers in bad times and the last to be added in good times. "'I would love to think they (interest rates) would continue to go down but I think it's temporary,' said William Pirtle, Merchandising Vice President for Lazarus department stores, a 16-store chain based in Columbus, Ohio. 'I think that business in big-ticket items, and I'm including furniture, will continue to be difficult through 1983.'" Not every one of the other 36,000 buyers that attended the market agreed with Pirtle, but many did and remained wary. The outcome was "particularly important to North Carolina, where about 600 plants employing some 84,000 workers, produce 25% of the nation's furniture." Employment was down for

---
58   "Furniture Makers Plan Earlier Show", CO, May 17, 1982, p. 5C.
59   Peter W. Barnes, "Furniture Mart Opens Amid Some Optimism", CO, October 19, 1982, p. 13A.

the state's industry, which boasted furniture as one of its three big industries at the time, along with textiles and tobacco. The previous year just under 5,000 people had been laid off in factories around NC. Just before the market opened the number had jumped to almost 8,000.[60]

Industry insider and president of Century Furniture Company, Hickory's largest, Harley Shuford, Jr. took a wait and see attitude saying it was too early to expect retailers to jump back in and buy like they had in markets before. "It's been a long struggle for some of the people. They (furniture retailers) are going to have to see some concrete good news for an extended period." Noting that the wheel had begun to turn, he said, "They're certainly more receptive to looking at new things," which was an improvement. "A few months ago they might have said, why, we won't even go look.'"[61]

Looking for a competitive advantage in a tight economic market where they were not even the biggest player, the western manufacturers and their showroom allies sought to play to their strengths. One advantage they noticed was upholstery. According to one account, "few retailers can afford to bypass the west, where upholstered furniture showrooms are concentrated. Most dealers will be hard pressed to miss Bernhardt, Century or Broyhill exhibits - just to name three." However, upholstery was not a savior. "Hickory can claim barely a fourth of all the exhibition space in the sprawling Southern Furniture Market, and the focus of the twice-yearly exposition remains keyed on High Point and its Southern Furniture Market Center, the market's largest showroom." The facts

---

60   Peter W. Barnes, "Furniture Mart Opens Amid Some Optimism", CO, October 19, 1982, p. 13A.
61   Peter W. Barnes, "Furniture Mart Opens Amid Some Optimism", CO, October 19, 1982, p. 13A.

spelled trouble for Hickory. Its largest displayer, Hickory Furniture Mart could be a casualty if all business went east to High Point.

"Now, western area exhibitors are employing savvy marketing techniques to publicize their niche in the show. They include new posters and special mailing campaigns." In the effort to get furniture buyers to think of the west as an important stop in the their buying and not just an 'add-on' to the must see showrooms, the two wings of furniture displays promised to unite for their common good. Observers had noticed that "before, exhibitors in the east and west operated more independently. Now, just as exhibitors in the west are cooperating on advertising and promotion with their eastern counterparts, western exhibitors are pooling their resources."[62]

In the west, wholesalers sought some stability after years of erratic opening day schedules. "Last market, for example, western makers said they would open their doors officially two days before exhibitors in the east," reported Peter Barnes of the Charlotte Observer. As Barnes explained, "previously, western exhibitors opened their showrooms to visiting retailers on an informal basis. But one showroom might open Monday, while another would open Tuesday and a third on Wednesday. That could make shopping difficult for dealers who intend to get all of their visiting in the west done at one time." These were the days before cell phones and the internet, when buyers wrote out their schedule on paper and wanted to be sure their showroom would be open when they came calling.

Everyone in the west pitched in to help. They knew that if the un-

---

62 Peter Barnes, "Exhibitors Promote Western Furniture Market", CO, April 17, 1983, Catawba Valley Neighbors Section, p. 14.

thinkable happened, and the Furniture Market no longer visited Hickory, everyone would suffer. To accommodate the early arrivals, the Catawba County Chamber of Commerce set up a housing bureau to find lodging beyond the standard hotel rooms in the area. According to one report, "more than 500 retailing firms sought rooms for their buyers through the bureau for the current market, up about 100 from last April."[63]

The effort to be more responsive to the needs of the wholesale crowd had been spearheaded by Hickory Furniture Mart. Spending $250,000 on a computer system two years earlier, the Mart could provide "mailings and promotions for itself and the area's two other major showrooms, the Hickory Merchandise Mart and the Hickory Home Furnishings Mart. Together, the three showrooms house about 180 furniture exhibitors." With some 30,000 retailers in their database, HFM pepper them with letters and fliers about Furniture Mart events, including opening dates for all their companies. In addition, the names came with numbers and could be followed up with a phone call. "That little personal touch, I think, is the answer to it," says Jack Sheer, Sales Manager for Hickory Leather Co. of nearby Vale, in Lincoln County." Of the 35 contacts he made by phone, a majority (25) said they would try to drop by his showroom at the Mart. As Sheer concluded, "The phone call kind of puts the lid on it."

Hickory Furniture Mart even commissioned the design of a poster that accented the area's edge in upholstery. The market poster "which has been in high demand, depicts the silhouette of a woman standing behind an armchair in a background of red print fabric. The idea, says G.

---

63   Peter Barnes, "Exhibitors Promote Western Furniture Market", CO, April 17, 1983, Catawba Valley Neighbors Section, p. 14.

Leroy Lail, President of the Mart, is to suggest that "fashion is furniture and furniture is fashion."[64]

The link between furniture and fashion had been a topic of HFM conversation for some time. Its realization came when Quaker Fabric Corp. followed Trend Line and Montclair, locating their "showroom and offices at the Hickory Furniture Mart." in 1983. While the corporate office for the company remained in Falls River, Massachusetts, the company permanently housed three of it is sales representatives out of the Mart, as well as showrooms. They were not alone. Quaker joined "Collins and Aikman, La France Industries, Malden Mills and Mastercraft Fabrics." who had already moved to the Mart. "The Quaker offices will be in a remodeled section of the Mart which includes offices of the Upholstery Forum - a fact-gathering, information-disseminating group for the furniture industry."[65] As wholesale buying was changing, so was Hickory Furniture Mart.

When new furniture companies sprang up, as they often did, the Hickory Furniture Mart was their showroom outlet. Take, for example Andre Teague, who started Dunmore Furniture in 1983. He found an old factory building used by Maxwell Royal in Hickory and began producing upholstery there in the summer of 1983. He immediately went to the Hickory Furniture Mart to market Dunmore's samples for the Fall Southern Furniture Market in October. The move gave Teague immediate access to the wholesale market and allowed Dunmore the opportunity to rack up orders as it was gearing up its operation."[66]

---

64   Peter Barnes, "Exhibitors Promote Western Furniture Market", CO, April 17, 1983, Catawba Valley Neighbors Section, p. 14.
65   "Quaker To Move To Mart", CO, June 23, 1983, Catawba Valley Neighbors Section, p. 9.
66   Karen Barber, "New Furniture Maker Finds Home in Old Factory, CO, September 4,

Amidst the maelstrom of changes in the furniture world, numerous new companies moved to the Mart. First time exhibitors for the fall of 1983 included "Bushline Corp. of Tazewell, Tenn., Computer Alternatives, of Hickory; Continental Chair of Hickory, Dunmore Furniture Industries Inc. of Hickory; Executive House, a division of Slumber Perfect Product of Hulk, Miss.' Grant Park of Atlanta; Far East Furniture Galleries of Landing, N.J.; Paul Robert Chair Co. of Taylorsville, and Washington Furniture of Houlka, Miss."[67]

As late as the fall of 1983, showroom operators express optimism of good markets and a rosy future for them in Hickory. "Glenn Lawrence, President of DeVille Furniture Co. in Hickory, said that although retailers are using reduced-price promotions to coax buyers, they are "very upbeat" about sales prospects for the year. Most industry observers predict 10% to 12% growth industrywide in furniture sales for the next 12 months, Lawrence said at his showroom in the Hickory Furniture Mart."[68]

Then came the tipping point. In the spring of 1984 when several western end companies moved their showrooms to High Point, two pivotal makers took different positions on leaving Hickory. Broyhill announced they intended to stay saying they were "optimistic about its continued success in the west." Gene Gunter, President of Broyhill admitted that "we have been observing the trend" but did not want to pull the rug out from the area that supported the company with its labor. He said, "the money the western market brings in is extremely important to the total community, and it would have been better for some of the other manufacturers

---

1983, Catawba Valley Neighbors Section (CVN), p. 8.
67   "New Companies Exhibiting At Markets", CO, Catawba Valley Neighbors (CVN), p. 9.
68   Diane St. John, "Furniture Makers Approach Market With Optimism", CO, October 19, 1983, p. 15A.

(if they had stayed)." Gunter put it in its simplest terms by observing that "every one (manufacturer) here is a drawing card, and every time you add one, it enhances the attraction of the west. And every time you remove one, the attraction of the west diminishes somewhat. Had they remained, the attractiveness would have been greater. But they left and now we're going to have to market our product aggressively to offset that." Buck Shuford of Century Furniture "stopped short of saying his company will relocate in High Point" but conceded they were going "to look at the situation very carefully."[69]

The trend had begun several years earlier as market observers noticed buyers spending less time in Hickory during the market. Shuford remarked, "over the past four or five years, fewer and fewer of our customers have stayed in Hickory. Most of our customers (now) stay for one day - they drive over for one day (from High Point). It becomes a question of how long these people are going to take one day to see relatively few people in the west."[70]

The situation had become apparent to everyone. The spring market of 1984 found the Hickory Home Furnishings Mart, which had changed its name to Home Resource Center to broaden its appeal, had "about 40,000-square-feet empty. Lane and North Hickory had already announced plans to leave, but still held space. Meanwhile, both the Hickory Furniture Mart and the Merchandise Mart, now managed by Leroy Lail, were still at full capacity, but the handwriting was on the wall. North Carolina's semi-annual furniture show no longer included a drive be-

---

69   Karen Barber, "The Big Boys", CO, April 19, 1984, Catawba Valley Neighbors (CVN), p. 4.
70   Karen Barber, "The Big Boys", CO, April 19, 1984, CVN, p. 4.

tween High Point and Hickory."[71]

The advantages of a one-city shopping stop for furniture retailers was obvious. In the east, over 1,200 showrooms waited to greet buyers, while the western end offered only 130. Alex Bernhardt put it succinctly. By moving to his company's new 42,000 square feet of display space he expected "a dramatic increase in traffic." High Point claimed 80% of the available 5 million square feet of showrooms, perused by visitors each market.

With such an advantage Hickory, as well as Lenoir and Morganton stood to lose the big economic boost the market brought twice yearly. At the Hickory Furniture Mart, a few last ditch attempts were made to accommodate the buyers coming to High Point. The mart set up "a shuttle service between High Point and Hickory" to save retailers the chore of driving. The van offered rides "on a first-come, first-served basis."[72] While in Hickory, guests were treated lavishly, with parties and activities galore. In addition to a "Hickory Buyer Cocktail Buffet," "tennis, racquetball, golf, and bowling tournaments" were organized as well as a "Joggers Fun Run" and a run for the more experienced, a "3.1-mile competition." Festivities concluded with an "All-Industry Mexican Fiesta" at Hickory Furniture Mart, for guests of the furniture show.[73]

Hickory did not give up without a fight. Looking for its niche and ready to promote it, billboards went up along Interstate 40 that claimed Hickory was the "Nation's Upholstery Center." By that point, Hickory Furniture Mart's Public Relations Director Burr Thompson, had rolled out a "national advertising campaign in which major retailers tout Hickory and

---

71   Karen Barber, "Home Resource Center Diversifies", CO, April 19, 1984, CVN, p. 5.
72   "Furniture Shuttle", CO, March 22, 1984, CVN, p. 10.
73   "Furniture Buyers Can Mix Business With Fun", CO, April 19, 1984, CVN, p. 9.

Lenoir as the upholstery center of the nation." The campaign included ads in furniture trade magazines as well as "mass promotional mailings to thousands of buyers."[74]

While the exodus became apparent to the public around 1984, industry insiders in the west saw the changes coming for a while. Leroy Lail claimed nothing had really changed on the western end. Reports quoted him as saying "the specialty we chose was in (exhibiting) the medium-priced upholstery goods." "We have never changed," he said. But he did acknowledge that "about three years ago, we started saying, 'OK, what is it we can do to the trade to let them know what we are doing?'" And the promotional campaign was born.[75]

As some furniture makers headed east, the space created opportunity for others. A small company in Hiddenite, making "early American, traditional and transitional furniture" finally found an opportunity to exhibit at the Hickory Furniture Mart. R.D. Johnson sought for a year to get a slot but was unsuccessful, until the spring 1984 market. Johnson was looking for the same thing at Hickory Furniture Mart that Alex Bernhardt sought in moving to High Point, traffic. Johnson had one retailer that kept his company, Red Barn Furniture, busy but he was seeking opportunities to expand his operation and showing at the market gave him entry into a world to which he had never previously had access. Red Barn became one of nine new exhibitors "leasing space previously occupied by manufacturers who moved from western showrooms to High Point since the October market."[76]

---

74   Karen Barber, "Campaign Touts Hickory as Upholstery Market", CO, April 19, 1984, CVN, p. 8.
75   Karen Barber, "Campaign Touts Hickory as Upholstery Market", CO, April 19, 1984, CVN, p. 8.
76   Diane St. John, "Furniture Exhibited to Attract Customers, CO, April 25, 1984, p.

The loss of the Southern Furniture Market was devastating to the region. No longer were hotels and motels filled to capacity, restaurants did not do overflow business each April and October, there were no temp jobs to shuttle buyers from one place to another. Catering and entertainment businesses had to look elsewhere for engagements. Plus, the showrooms, that were once so full began to see their space empty out. However, in the wake of the crushing loss of business, new opportunity arose.

The summer of 1984 began to reveal a new business model that would be the savior to Hickory's rich history of furniture making. With a 50-acre complex that included a motel and restaurant, as well as the Hickory Furniture Mart, Leroy Lail had been "looking for a thread to link the businesses." On the property was also a drive-in theater and bank. "A retail outlet is about the only thing we were really missing," said Lail in a 1984 interview. He continued, "so we added it." After years of scheduling the furniture Mart for other events during its down time, he began to add to the complex with a variety of new businesses. First came Hickory Furniture Connection, a "home and office furniture retailer representing more than 300 lines of furniture and accessories." Then came Northwest Passage, "an accessories retailer and wholesaler featuring Asian imports" which also carried "some furniture." A retail clothier was also part of the new lineup.

According to a newspaper report, Lail had been developing the idea since 1977, seven years earlier. John Schenk, Vice President of Hickory Furniture Mart said they had been very intentional about the way they chose the new storefronts, adding "we want them to accent the motel and the Furniture Market." The association with the Hickory Furniture Mart

A19.

would soon have some very beneficial connections but at the start, it may have hampered business. Initially, the manager of the Hickory Furniture Connection, Nancy Holmes admitted that "a lot of people see this building connected with the furniture Mart and can't buy furniture here." She was counting on word getting out that a change was in process. She added, "but I think as people become aware of the fact that we're open to the public, things will really pick up."[77]

The entire complex was being redeveloped. Lail planned to push the retail concept even further, adding "another 6,000 to 8,000 square feet" for more shops. In addition to adding a "63-room expansion to the motel" a 60,000 square foot office building was considered. The retail village being created would attract shoppers who were already traveling down Highway 64/70 as a result of Valley Hills Mall locating just up the street and the fact that "many of the customers who stay at Mull's Motel are moving to the Hickory area and need furniture and clothing."[78]

For a while, the losses in the wholesale market were made up by new tenants. Floor space at the Hickory Furniture Mart had expanded to 400,000 square feet. Those who moved to High Point left a 30,000 square foot hole but the deficit was quickly made up with 18 new exhibitors, allowing Leroy Lail to say, "so far, it looks like a very normal market."[79] But in reality, it was not a normal market. Reports called the market "meager" and noted that there was no problem finding parking at any of the furniture showrooms in Hickory.[80] The first casualty was the Home Resource Center, which was at only about 30% capacity during the fall

---

77 Liz Chandler, "The Missing Link", CO, June 28, 1984, CVN, p. 8.
78 Liz Chandler, "The Missing Link", CO, June 28, 1984, CVN, p. 8.
79 Diane St. John, "Furniture Retailers Buying Optimistically", CO, p. 10A.
80 Diane St. John, "Attendance Meager at Furniture Market", October 18, 1984, p. 15A.

show.[81]

The retail idea, initially planned for space outside the Hickory Furniture Mart penetrated the building. At the end of the market Hickory Leather did not pack up its samples as it, and every other furniture maker had done at the market. With "more than 55 chairs, loveseats and other pieces in their 3,600-square-foot showroom, they kept "their exhibit open all year long for consumer as well as professional buyers."[82]

Scott Lail observed that his father took the changes very much in stride. He said, "dad, he did not seem particularly stressed out to me. Granted, I was in Chapel Hill and he wasn't around, but he would interact with me. He just did not seem all that stressed out to me when everybody did pick up and leave and we converted." For Leroy Lail, change did not mean loss, it meant opportunity. Scott Lail agreed. "I think because he knew in his mind what he wanted to do and knew how to plan and felt pretty confident that the plan was solid and it was going to work and it has." Leroy Lail's oldest son recognized in his father the ability to promote the new plan and through that promotion make it work so that, his knack for "promoting the building and getting people to want to drive to Hickory to buy furniture" would continue.[83]

By the end of the year, the Mart announced plans to open year round, at least partially. In addition to the retail showroom of Hickory Leather, the East Atrium would be devoted to interior design facilities. The step reflected the changing times in the furniture business. John Schenk noted that "we have retailers visiting Hickory at times other than the market," and sought to accommodate them "by maintaining year-

---

81 William Mills, "Large Sales Expected at Hickory Furniture Market", CO, p. 7A.
82 Diane St. John, "Some Hickory Furniture Exhibitors to Remain Open", CO, p. 6C.
83 Interview with Scott Lail, Hickory Furniture Mart, September 2, 2020.

round showroom facilities, since not all buying is done at market."[84]

While the Hickory Furniture Mart was evolving into a new type of furniture buying experience, the other two showrooms in Hickory converted rather quickly into other operations. The old Hickory Home Furnishings Mart on Highway 321 was sold to CommScope, a cable producer looking to establish its corporate headquarters in Hickory. The next day, the Hickory Merchandise Mart announced it would convert its 100,000 square feet of display space into offices. Leroy Lail by this time, with several partners, controlled the Merchandise Mart and decided to "accelerate his diversification plans" after he learned of the Siecor move. Saying "the demand for corporate office space was greater than we had anticipated," he pointed out that "real estate is a good investment." The moves in the spring of 1985 allowed the Hickory Furniture Mart to funnel all those manufacturers who were displaying at the other two Hickory locations to come to the one remaining showroom for furniture.[85]

In the press, Leroy Lail was quoted as predicting the Furniture Market, long a part of the Hickory economy would be irrelevant. "In the next five years," Lail said, " the show will be even less important. We'll have a lot more year-round markets."[86] Pinkney Hull agreed. As President of Hickory Leather, the first year round furniture tenant, he was pleased with the chance to open his doors to "designers, dealers and other customers." He observed that the new arrangement "gives the same atmosphere as you get during market. They can look at a picture and be told

---

84 "Hickory Mart To Open Year Round", CO, CVN, p. 16.
85 Karen Barber and Tammy Joyner, "Hickory Loses 2nd Mart To Offices", CO, April 11, 1985, p. 23A; Tammy Joyner, "Hickory Broadens Its Base As Furniture Market Shifts", CO, April 28, 1985, p. 6B, 12B.
86 Karen Barber and Tammy Joyner, "Hickory Loses 2nd Furniture Mart To Offices", CO, April 11, 1985, p. 1, 12.

what the furniture looks like, but these buyers like to kick the tires, so to speak."[87]

Though the other two display facilities had given up on furniture, Leroy Lail believed that the industry was still very much a part of Hickory and would attract a more evergreen customer. Observing that "because of the concentration of furniture manufacturers in the area," Hickory would always be connected to furniture and by recognizing the changes in the buying and selling process, Hickory could benefit. In fact, the Hickory Furniture Mart had already diversified substantially from it origins back in 1960. Of the Mart's floor space totaling 350,000 square feet, year round exhibition space totaled between 20,000 and 30,000 square feet in early 1985, while another 50,000 square feet were devoted to corporate offices and fabric showrooms. The transformation was picking up speed.[88]

When Broyhill made its decision known to pack up their Lenoir showroom and exhibit only in High Point, the Hickory Furniture Mart was left as the only western place for buyers to come. Figuring that wholesale shoppers spent on average, $133 per day and up to 2,500 came to see the company's wares, Lenoir stood to lose over $100,000 dollars in revenue. The same prospect loomed even larger for Catawba County where more manufacturers still hoped to attract customers in the semi-annual show.[89]

By the fall of 1985 "about 40 exhibitors" were part of the twice-yearly wholesale show, with all of them at the Hickory Furniture Mart. Clearly, the balance had fully tipped to High Point and Hickory

---

87 Karen Barber, "Year-Round Showrooms Mark Future", CO, CVN, p. 13.
88 Karen Barber, "Year-Round Showrooms Mark Future", CO, CVN, p. 13.
89 Liz Chandler, "Firms Say Lost Showroom Means Lost Business", CO, April 21, 1985, CVN, p. 14.

was seeing the end of its career as a furniture buyers' market. As some local companies had been acquired by larger names, the decision to move came from outside the area. For example, Bassett now owned both Impact in Icard and Montclair in Claremont, both of which had shown in Hickory. The parent company announced their move.[90]

While the decline struck fear in the hearts of many in Hickory, Leroy Lail refrained from such worry. In contrast, he was downright optimistic. Recognizing the market was changing, Lail offered, "people like myself need to be responsive to what's happening today. Our business is constantly responding to changes in the marketplace." Lail called the conversion of a twice-yearly market into a year round endeavor a step forward for Hickory.[91] Ultimately, he was right, but at the time many doubted it. Their problems centered around the fact that they lacked the vision of Leroy Lail.

The conversion of Hickory from a wholesalers market into a retail buying space had begun. But as it evolved, there were still events scheduled at the Hickory Furniture Mart to fill in the gap. Still connected to the furniture industry, the Mart continued to host a Furniture Industry Exposition, a chance for suppliers to show the factory owners the latest in products that help make furniture. After the conversion of the Hickory Merchandise Mart to office space, the event moved to the Hickory Furniture Mart which allowed for almost three times the floor space and thus many more vendors. The 1986 event also was the first to fully flip the paradigm for furniture makers. Instead of them offering pieces to retail-

---

90   Karen Barber," "Market Weeks Play Smaller Role For Hickory Market", CO, October 17, 1985, CVN, p. 14.
91   Karen Barber," "Market Weeks Play Smaller Role For Hickory Market", CO, October 17, 1985, CVN, p. 14.

ers, they were the buyers coming to Hickory to see what suppliers could offer. Brent Kincaid, Vice President for Procurement at Broyhill Furniture Industries liked the way it worked. "It's an opportunity to take a total look at the supplier market in a short period of time," something retailers had said in the same building years earlier about the furniture companies. Now Broyhill was was one of several thousand manufacturers coming to see what the 153 suppliers from across the country could offer to make his product better.[92]

Among the very last to leave the market was Conover's Southern Furniture. In the spring of 1986 the company announced its intention to show only in High Point. For a year, Southern maintained showrooms in both locations, but the pull was too great. "Inevitable" was how Jerome Bolick, president of Southern Furniture described the move. He was quoted as saying "we are the only ones left over here; I don't know of anyone else showing in the area." Bolick had watched as all his competitors had moved to High Point, reporting larger numbers of visitors to their showrooms and predictably, larger sales as a result. By the time Southern made its exit, the FFMAS, sponsor of the Southern Furniture Market, had closed its offices in Hickory. Executive Director Richard Barentine said, "it was time."[93]

By then, the Hickory Furniture Mart said goodbye to twice annual events and hello to a 360 day per year orientation. The idea that instead of the frenzy of ten days in April and October, customers would visit throughout the year. And those customers would be both wholesal-

---

[92] Karen Barber, "Furniture Industry Exposition Starts Friday", CO, February 6, 1986, CVN, p. 9.
[93] Karen Barber, "Furniture Market: Hello, High Point, Goodbye, Hickory", CO, April 9, 1986, CVN, p. 9.

ers buying for their retail outlets as well as the public looking for a good deal on pieces made in the area. There had always been opportunities to buy furniture directly from the factory if one was an employee or knew someone who was, thus the popular belief was born that furniture was less expensive if bought near the spot of its manufacture.

Now, Hickory Furniture Mart played off that idea with the growing array of retailers, which included the manufacturers themselves, and could offer wholesale prices to the public. One company with showrooms in the Hickory Furniture Mart advertised that they were "headquartered in the heart of the Furniture Capital of the World (still a slogan in use)" and they brought those prices "directly" to shoppers. Far East Galleries advertised, "At Last...Affordable Custom Furniture," adding that buyers could have it their way by choosing "Fabric, Style Finish, all at Factory Direct Prices." Many other companies advertised in much the same mode.[94]

Soon, the news in town was not what was leaving, but what was coming. Announcements began to fill the papers about the next new tenant at the Hickory Furniture Mart. A diversity of home furnishings options became available. In September American Custom Unfinished Furniture opened their showroom at the Design Center. The three year old company offered a variety of solid oak pieces including suites for both bedroom and dining room, as well as occasional chairs and roll-top desks. China Sea Trader advertised a variety of unique pieces for decoration.[95]

A unique addition to furniture related activities borne out of the new Hickory Furniture Mart came with the announcement of a "Furniture Festival for the spring of 1987. Leroy Lail said the idea had been

---
94 Far East Galleries (advert), CO, September 12, 1986, p. 14A.
95 "Headquarters Open", CO, September 14, 1986, CVN, p. 8; "Cloisonne Horses" (advert), CO, September 15, 1986, p. 12A.

"discussed for some time, and we feel there is a need to have a festival to focus on Hickory's history and heritage in furniture." The event included a week of activities with seminars, lectures, demonstrations and a "fashion and furniture show."[96]

A week later, an advertisement appeared entreating shoppers to "pick up a real bargain." The Hickory Furniture Mart announced "the biggest furniture clearance ever," as part of a fall market samples show and sale. As a logical extension of the wholesale market days, the ad could have been a leftover from the days when Hickory welcomed buyers from all over the country and in the aftermath a huge clearance of samples were now available for public purchase. But with the Southern Furniture Market clearly gone, this sale heralded a new incarnation for the Hickory Furniture Mart.

Now the Hickory Furniture Mart was a host for retail outlets. Collectively, they were advertising as a year-round market where the manufacturers (and others) were selling directly to the public. In the initial ad, sixteen companies offered "unbelievable savings" with "prices sacrificed." The announcement also contained the promise of even greater choice with "many new galleries added" alerting buyers that other companies were setting up shop.[97]

As the mart began to fill up with retailers, there was still room for specialty shows. "Blowing Rock's Art in the Park craft show will produce Art in the Atrium at the Hickory Furniture Mart." The show offered participating artists and craftsmen an opportunity to display their work, within a juried show, just as the Blowing Rock Chamber of Commerce

---

96 "Hickory Furniture Festival Announced", CO, October 19, 1986, CVN, p. 13.
97 "The Biggest Furniture Clearance Sale Ever" (advert), CO, October 26, 1986, p. 21A.

had been doing in the resort town for over two decades. "In our 22 years, this will be the first time we have ever 'come off the mountain,' and we are thrilled," commented the Chamber's Dixie Hoffland. The event demonstrated the varied approach to offering customers a unique setting to furnish their homes. The array included stained glass, oil paintings, wood carvings and wall hangings, all available for purchase.[98]

Additionally, furniture stores within the Mart also advertised their offerings individually. In one unique move, the Hickory Furniture Connection and Hickory Furniture Galleries teamed up to stage a "Leather Furniture Sale." Coaxing shoppers with the invitation to "warm up to the beauty of leather" the two companies were able to do something they never would have been able to accomplish in individual storefronts. Their partnering drew visitors who also might peek into other stores, creating traffic and getting the word out that Hickory Furniture Mart was now a retail establishment.[99]

A flood of special events were held to promote the Hickory Furniture Mart. Christmas shows, moving sales, anything that could draw a crowd was planned and promoted. When American Heritage Distributors moved from one space in the Mart to another, they had a moving sale, saying they "would rather sell it than move it." [100]

When the suppliers show rolled around in early 1987, the event proved to be so popular that spaces were sold out. A number of new companies hoping to gain the attention of furniture makers boosted the popularity of the show, including several exhibits from companies in

---
98 "Blowing Rock to Do Art, Craft Show in Hickory", CO, October 31, 1986, p. CVN, p. 8; "Art in the Atrium" (advert), CO, November 9, 1986, p. 30A.
99 "Leather Furniture Sale" (advert), Asheville Citizen-Times, November 20, 1986, p. 2.
100 "Christmas Show" (advert), CO, November 23, 1985, CVN, p. 11-12; "Moving Sale" (advert), CO, December 3, 1986, p. 7B.

High Point. Reporter Karen Barber called it "a scene reminiscent of the semiannual Southern Furniture Market in Hickory before manufacturers began the showroom exodus to High Point. One hundred-fifty suppliers, presenting more than 350 product lines welcomed over 2,000 perspective customers in the 3 day event."[101]

The suppliers show provided an important service to the furniture industry. It gave manufacturers a chance to see not only what was available to help them make furniture, it also gave producers a taste of what was new and innovative. Bob Bush, Vice President of Hickory Springs Manufacturing was impressed with the turnout and the interest. "We were busy constantly - even on Saturday morning, which is usually deadsville," he observed. Citing somewhere near 40% of visitors expressing interest in the components Hickory Springs had to offer, he acknowledged that he did gain some orders, but also pointed out that "we're trying to show what's new."[102]

In addition to the suppliers show, the Mart sponsored a furniture festival to highlight the heritage of manufacturing and what it has brought to the area. In 1987, the year of the first festival, Catawba County still claimed over 15,000 people working in the industry, over 20% of the county's workforce. Leroy Lail sought to present an homage to the many people who toiled in the area's factories, at that point an industry that had been around for almost a century. Their products had gone all over the nation as well as the world, as ornaments to people's homes. He also envisioned a museum to begin the process of documenting the evolution

---

101   "Organization News" News & Observer (Raleigh), January 29, 1987, p. 8B; "Show Space Sells Out", CO, January 11, 1987, CVN, p, 9; Karen Barber, "Furniture Suppliers Put on Big Show", CO, CVN, p. 8.
102   Karen Barber, "Furniture Suppliers Put on Big Show", CO, CVN, p. 8.

of the process over the years. With the Catawba County Historical Association, he developed a plan for presentation of the story. After helping to create a traveling exhibit on multipurpose furniture for the Smithsonian Institution, he admitted, "the reason I got involved was I had so many people ask me about furniture." Wanting to tell the story of furniture's development in the Catawba Valley, he found that the costs of housing such a museum would be "astronomical, we're talking about several million dollars to make a presentation." Instead, he found space within the Hickory Furniture Mart to develop the idea. "Before we can have a national scope, we need to crawl inch-by-inch first," he said.

The festival had many components. The local community college's furniture production program demonstrated the process of making an upholstered piece. Also, local artists gave talks on their expertise. Chair caning, furniture painting (chinoiserie), and tapestry weaving were just a few of the events at the festival. Tenants within the Mart also offered special prices during the two-day event.[103]

One of the busiest advertisers within the Hickory Furniture Mart was Far East Galleries. The company had two locations, one in Charlotte, the other in the Mart. One bold headline in their regular campaign of advertisements read, "We'd Like To Tell You Where To Go." Within it, they explained how to get to the Mart to see their "10,000 square foot store." The ad used nearby Valley Hills Mall as a reference, stating "If you've never heard of Far East Galleries, chances are you've never seen it and more likely you don't know how to get there. We'd like to change that. The advertisement included a map showing their proximity along High-

---

103   Karen Barber, "Furniture Festival To Show heritage", CO, May 13, 1987, CVN, p. 9.

way 64-70 as a way to spot the Mart and their location within it.[104] Far East Galleries represented a second generation of furniture entrepreneurs within shouting distance of Hickory.

The roots of the Catawba Valley Furniture making tradition are long. For so many companies in Hickory Furniture Mart, they show up regularly. David Bolick proudly revealed his. His grandfather, Charles Sr. was part of the workforce at nearby Conover's Southern Furniture, Jerome Bolick's company that was among the last to leave. Later, David Bolick's father Charles, Jr. started his own company, Alexvale Furniture. Like Kim Sigmon and countless others, the younger Bolick turned family tradition into sales, starting Hickory Park Furniture Galleries as Far East Cargo, then Far East Galleries, before rebranding for a final time. Each incarnation of the business has brought in customers and now with "nearly 90,000 square feet of indoor and outdoor furniture and accessory options in every style and price point, including some of North Carolina's most well-known furniture manufacturers, Hickory Park remains one of Hickory Furniture Mart's longest retail tenants.[105] Within two years, the younger Bolicks opened a second store in the Hickory Furniture Mart.[106]

Eventually, the suppliers show was forced out of the Hickory Furniture Mart, due to space. By the time the show was ready to stage its eighth annual event, the Mart had grown its permanent showroom space for retailers to the point that room for the suppliers was limited. Even though the Mart contained over five acres of available footage, "most of that space (was) used for permanent displays," said Cindy Beason of

---

104   "We'd Like To Tell You Where To Go." (advert), CO, March 8, 1987, CVN, p. 11.
105   "Hickory Park Furniture Galleries", Hickory Furniture Mart: The Magazine: 47th Buying Guide Edition, p. 42.
106   Rob Urban, "Furniture Business Doing So Well That Owner Decides To Expand", CO, October 30, 1987, CVN, p. 9.

HFM. As President of Hickory Mart Shows, who put on the event, Leroy Lail saw registrations for the the 1988 show were going to be "at least 15% larger" than the previous year's. He said, "with this kind of continuing expansion we had to look beyond stopgap measures toward a permanent solution. So the Furniture Suppliers Show moved to a location across town called (at the time) Country Adventures.[107]

It's not that the Hickory Furniture Mart was not growing, it was. By the fall of 1987 another 70,000-square-feet of showroom space had been added. It's just that as soon as the new area came on line, it was rented to a plethora of new tenants. Pennsylvania House, Rhoney Furniture House, and Piedmont Designs of Hickory were just some of the companies that vied for space in the increasingly popular Mart. Perhaps more popular than the days of the wholesale buyer, the Hickory Furniture Mart was now synonymous with furniture buying in the retail market.[108]

Small one and two day shows became a staple at the Mart toward the end of the 80s. the "Carolina Christmas Show" highlighted everything for the yuletide season, while International Tours presented a one-day cruise show for those interested in taking such a vacation jaunt, complete with a fashion show on what to wear and films on where to go. The expo also offered a raffle for a free three-day cruise.[109]

While the Hickory Furniture Mart welcomed those visiting, Mart personnel were also out aggressively seeking new events to bring to Hickory. Marketing Director Carol Cartledge ventured to numerous sites including Washington, DC as part of the Travel Council of North Carolina's

---

107   Greg Trevor, "Furniture Suppliers Show Moving to Larger Site", CO, October 21, 1987, CVN, p. 8.
108   "New Showroom Space", CO November 8, 1987, CVN, p. 17.
109   "Christmas Show", CO, November 14, 1987, CVN, p. 5; "Cruise Show", CO, January 29, 1988, CVN, p. 6.

effort to attract new business. Cartledge met with various travel association executives with the intent to bring new trade to Hickory.[110] Leroy Lail went even farther. In late 1987, he and his wife Lynn traveled to London as part of a "five-day mission sponsored by Piedmont Airlines, the N.C. Department of Commerce and the Charlotte Convention and Visitors Bureau to lure tourists to North Carolina." The group was filled with luminaries from the Tarheel state including Hugh Morton of Grandfather Mountain and former senator James T. Broyhill. The Hickory Furniture Mart was part of a contingent that also represented Old Salem, Biltmore House and the Charlotte Motor Speedway.[111]

Quickly, the Design Center became the hub of activity for the Furniture Mart. At the end of 1987, with approximately 17,000 square feet added that year, a number of new tenants gobbled up the space for their businesses. Resource Design found that after starting almost a year and a half earlier, their business "just grew and grew and grew" said Terry Silver, owner. "We started expanding until we expanded right out of the space we had," she commented, making the case for the expansion of her company that carried a variety of fabrics for the home. Among the other new companies was Piedmont Designs which occupied 6,000 square feet.[112]

The Design Center created substantial excitement in several ways. First, as a source for ideas to furnish interior spaces, "it's the logical place to be for anyone in the furnishings related field," said Lynn Lail, owner of Piedmont Designs. As she noted, "so many designers come through

---

110   "Promoting Tourism", CO, November 25, 1987, p. CVN, p. 9.
111   "Southern Hospitality", CO, December 9, 1987, CVN, p. 12.
112   Beverly Brown, "Hickory Furniture Design Center Gets New Tennants", CO, December 27, 1987, CVN, p. 14.

here and it's open year-round." Promotions provided another stimulating reason to shop. In January of 1988, an Asheville couple won a trip for two to Hawaii as part of a design center promotion.[113]

In a variety of ways, the Mart became a cultural center for the Hickory community, as well as the business community in the late 80s. The Chamber held multiple business events there, including a "Business After Hours" reception when the City of Hickory celebrated the anniversary of the council/manager form of government they installed 75 years earlier. Hickory, being the first in North Carolina and fourth in the nation, was early to adopt the administrative innovation and benefitted from it.[114]

Another public service provided by the Design Center was co-sponsorship of an education poster contest in conjunction with Catawba County Education Week. In 1988, the theme was "Stay in Power." Susan Hunsucker and Vivian Rogers, of Susan Hunsucker Gallery, in the Hickory Furniture Mart's Design Center, judged the entries. Winning posters were selected from all three of the county's school systems. A winner from each grade within each system were displayed at nearby Valley Hills Mall. The Furniture Mart's partner in the contest was the Catawba County Chamber of Commerce.[115]

Over the years, the Hickory Furniture Mart had seen a lot of changes. Still located next to the Mart was Mull's restaurant, with a history of its own. In the spring of 1988, the Design Center hosted a reception for Beckie Melton. Her service as a waitress for Mull's went back to the

---

113   Beverly Brown, "Hickory Furniture Design Center Gets New Tennants", CO, December 27, 1987, CVN, p. 14; "Center Awards Trip", CO, December 13, 1987, CVN, p. 4; "Couple Wins Trip to Hawaii", Asheville Citizen-Times, January 5, 1988, p. 47.
114   "After Hours Reception", CO, March 16, 1988, CVN, p. 12.
115   "Winners Announced In Education Poster Competition", CO, March 27, 1988, CVN, p. 12.

days when the establishment was known as Hickory Drive-In Restaurant. After starting in 1952, Melton worked there for 35 years, witnessing the creation of the Hickory Furniture Mart and its substantial growth. Saying she "found a good job and stuck with it," she acknowledged the many changes she saw at the complex. J.P. Mull tore down the original restaurant and built a 220-seat replacement in 1959, just before he created Hickory Furniture Mart.[116]

The Mart, now touted as a complex with over 5 acres of furniture on display, continued to expand. In the summer of 1988, the Design Center opened on Sunday afternoons. Since many furniture retailers were closed on Sunday, the new hours gave the center an additional feature "to meet customers" demands."[117]

The Design Center embodied many of the trends of furniture fashion and served through its stores within as a source for decorating, but the conformity brought one shop owner to open a store that catered to the individual. In fact, Ruth Fisher called her store, "One Of A Find." Established in the summer of 1988, Fisher dealt in "hard to find items" that she believed "appealed to designers and individuals." Her merchandise included "whimsical items, craft items made from wood, metal, clay, glass and other media; and some antiques." She also presented works of art from crafters located as far away as the mountains of western North Carolina.[118]

Business was going so well in the wake of the Furniture Market that the Design Center began construction of a four-level addition. The

---
116 "Waitress Honored", CO, May 25, 1988, CVN, p. 6; Beverly Brown, "Service With A Smile", Co, June 1, 1988, CVN, p. 8.
117 Peggy Beach, "Open on Sundays", CO, June 5, 1988, CVN, p. 21.
118 Peggy Beach, "Creative Accessories", CO, June 17, 1988, CVN, p. 9; "They Seek, Sell Unusual Accessories", CO, June 27, 1988, p. 4D.

new area added 40,000 square feet to the complex to accommodate an expected 300,000 visitors to the Mart in 1988. Leroy Lail believed "this demonstrates the viability and need in our market area," adding that he expected to complete the new area within five months.[119]

With growth at the furniture complex came growth within the leadership at the Mart. In the fall of 1988, John Schenk was promoted to President of the Design Center division of Hickory Furniture Mart. He succeeded Leroy Lail, who now took mantel as Chairman of the Board. Schenk had steadily worked his way up the ladder, starting at the Mart in 1972 while still a student at Lenoir-Rhyne College. He "joined the company full time after graduating in 1974, and was named Assistant Manager the following year. After jobs as Vice President within the organization, his ascension to the president's job heralded what Lail called "aggressive plans for growth." He added, "This promotion will afford us more flexibility in implementing these plans as the Design Center continues to add staff members."[120]

As time progressed, more of the retailers who left Hickory returned to set up shop of their own stores at the Furniture Mart. One was Larry Hendricks, owner of the Country Shop in Hickory. He opened a 10,000-square-foot Thomasville Gallery on the top level of the Mart in the fall of 1988. With "a full line of upholstered and wood furnishings by Thomasville," Hendricks' store demonstrated that furniture buying was back in Hickory, only in a slightly altered incarnation and not so dependent on a ten-day flurry each fall and spring.[121]

---

119   Beverly Brown, "Hickory's Design Center To build 4-Level Addition", CO, June 23, 1988, p. 7C.
120   "Hickory Furniture Names Design President", CO, September 18, 1988, CVN, p. 18.
121   "Thomasville Gallery", CO, October 16, 1988, CVN, p. 22.

Even with the Southern Furniture Market fleeing Hickory, the opportunity to capitalize on the hoopla, now in High Point, remained. Just as if the market were still visiting Hickory, the Design Center held an "After Market Sale," reporting that customers came from dozens of states. Mart officials labeled the sale a success, extending hours "in response to the growing popularity of the sale."[122] "When we first started having the After Market Sales, I remember that they were just tremendously successful," said Scott Lail. Noting that "we'd stand in the North courtyard and there would just be people everywhere," the sales heralded the growing importance of Hickory Furniture Mart as the region's most important retail location.[123]

As the square footage in the Hickory Furniture Mart continued to grow, so did the size of the stores within it. Reflections Contemporary Furniture was just one of the companies seeking more floor space. They added a leather gallery of 5,000 square feet, which pleased owner Giovanni Guidi. He said, "This expansion gives us the chance to display the finest lines of contemporary furniture, including bedroom, dining and living room, and to emphasize our strength in leather goods." For the tenants who located in the Mart, times were good and getting better.[124]

The diversity of attractions at the Mart only widened in the late 80s. For example, a Senior Citizens Fair invited the elderly to join in with an art exhibit and a checkers tournament. While there they could learn about a plethora of services offered "by local hospitals, colleges and other groups."[125] Historical groups got involved too as the Hickory Tavern Chap-

---

122 "After Market Sale", CO, November 27, 1988, CVN, p. 26.
123 Interview with Scott Lail, Hickory Furniture Mart, September 2, 2020.
124 "Furniture Store Grows", CO, February 5, 1989, CVN, p. 21.
125 "Senior Citizen Fair", CO, June 14, 1989, CVN, p. 19.

ter of the Daughters of the American Revolution gave away copies of the United States Constitution from from the lobby of HFM.[126]

Hickory Furniture Mart's address became a very fashionable one for a variety of new tenants, some in the furniture industry, some not. Conso Products, "the nation's largest manufacturer of decorative trimmings" opened its first North Carolina sales office at the Hickory Furniture Mart.[127] Northwood Furniture, manufacturer of upholstery announced locating a new store, Traditional Elegance at the HFM. Northwood Vice President John Wilson said, "I feel Hickory Furniture Mart has proven itself to be a vital consumer resource, and we see continued growth ahead in the decade of the '90s, with Northwood sharing in the growth."[128] Others agreed including many of the retail shops that once came during the market. Blowing Rock Chair, a furniture store between Hickory and Lenoir took space to display its
Broyhill Showcase Gallery.[129] It was not the only buyer that came back to create its own store.
Lexington Gallery leased 5000 square-feet for its showroom while Hickory White, one of Hickory's oldest companies returned with a gallery of 3500 square feet.[130]

It was all becoming rather crowded at HFM, even with the expanding space. Keeping up with promoting everything was handed over to a new advertising group. The Lyerly Agency was selected to promote the "more than 500 office and furniture lines" at HFM.[131] They had plenty

---

126 "Copy Of The Constitution", CO, July 2, 1989, CVN, p. 24.
127 "Conso Opens Office", CO, February 7, 1990, CVN, p. 13.
128 "Northwood Opens in Furniture Mart Design Center", CO, February 11, 1990, CVN, p. 29.
129 "Broyhill Store Planning to Open This Spring", CO, February 21, 1990, CVN, p. 12.
130 "2 Galleries Added", CO, April 11, 1990, CVN, p. 15.
131 "New Accounts", CO, April 23, 1990, p. 15C.

The parking lot of HFM soon after its conversion from wholesale to retail space. In the early days of the facility was billed as the "Design Center" and used the second version of Hickory Furniture Mart's leaf logo, which has been often copied.as the "Design Center" and used the second version of Hickory Furniture Mart's leaf logo, which has been often copied.the "Design Center" and used the second version of Hickory Furniture Mart's leaf logo, which has been often copied.

The first interior glass elevator in North Carolina. After seeing one in Atlanta, Leroy Lail decided Hickory Furniture Mart needed a way for visitor to see the vast expanse of shops on multiple floors. Part of the third addition to HFM.

Construction along Highway 70 for an addition around 1968. Notice the two lane road with the Esso gas station across the street. Also, the entrance to the Hickory Drive-In Theatre, part of the offerings at the Mull's Complex.

The front (or North Entrance to Hickory Furniture Mart. The completion of construction from the previous image, the new frontage offered a sleek new entrance to visitors to the Southern Furniture Market each April and October.

Letterhead created by Leroy Lail in 1972, along with the leaf logo. The design won awards for its innovative interplay between text and image. The design was created by John Malmo of Memphis.

The new HFM sign that utilizes the new version of the logo. The photo from around 2010 is the sign consumers are looking for when they drive to Hickory for discount prices on home furnishings.

One of the many parties held in the courtyard of the Mart. Beginning in 1965, Leroy Lail envisioned such a space, enlarging it with every addition. The courtyard made large gatherings possible for furniture related, as well as other gatherings.

Another view of the courtyard with a reception being held. The space worked well as a buffet dining space and allowed attendees to mingle as well as view the expanse of shops.

East entrance, addition from 1974. The entry doors included the bi-parted stairway that allowed manufacturing tenants to choose which floor they wanted to explore, a responsive solution to vendors concerns

A view of the four stories that look out onto the courtyard. A dazzling sight for customers seeking furniture choices upon their visit to HFM.

South entrance to HFM during one of the many expansions. Notice the temporary wall to the right that would later be filled in by a later addition.

Last construction project of the Mart. This image shows the massive addition on the southeastern corner of HFM. The new section replaced the temporary wall from the previous photo.

View from the interior courtyard at the south entrance. With four floors of shops, the use of glass to bring light into the building was a hallmark of Leroy Lail's design choices.

Leroy Lail and Sheldon Fineman at the celebration of HFM's twentieth anniversary. Notice the cake took the shape of the building in 1980. Fineman was one of a number of salesman that were important to the growth of HFM.

The Lail Family with new tenants to the Mart. From left, Leroy Lail (Chairman of the Board), Lynn Lail, Michael Duval, Brad Lail, Angie Cline, Scott Lail, Laura Lail Treadaway, and Tracey Trimble.

Reconstruction of the new (north) entrance to HFM, around 2002. Completed after the conversion of the Mart to a retail clientele.

Winners in a Hickory Furniture Mart sponsored tennis tournament. The court, added to the Mull's Complex was an important recreational feature that engaged furniture buyers during their time at the Mart as part of the Southern Furniture Market.

"Fashion Follows Furniture." This poster was one in a series that demonstrated the relationship of the two in furniture design. The poster won awards as an innovative way to promote HFM and were very popular.

The owners of Stylecraft Furniture, one of the early tenants of Hickory Furniture Mart. Owner George Brown and A. Austin are seen at a reception with one of their salesmen.

Aerial view of the south entrance at Hickory Furniture Mart.

Neighbors to the east of HFM. The former site of the Mull's Complex now houses Holiday Inn Express (forefront), with a variety of shops located in front. On the left is the east entrance to Hickory Furniture Mart.

Aerial view of adjacent businesses to the east of HFM with six-lane Highway 70 in front at the original site of Mull's Motel.

to promote. With fine art always a component of home decoration, it seemed fitting that The Catawba Visual Art League would find a place at the Mart. The League sponsored an "art exhibition and competition" with works on display at the HFM.[132]

Another important event that tied together the elements of Hickory Furniture Mart was a regional conference of the American Society of Interior Designers. The Carolina Chapter, which included Charlotte and Rock Hill, as well as Hickory, hosted the event with Michael Dugan, President of Henredon Furniture as the featured speaker. While "Dugan spoke on the culture of the 1990s and the economic impact of "baby boomers" on the home furnishing industry," he was also gathering data on the immense changes in the business of furniture. His experience would later lead him to a professorship at Lenoir-Rhyne College as well as authoring "Furniture Wars: How America Lost a Fifty Billion Dollar Industry" in 2009.[133]

For anyone doubting that HFM provided a central location for furnishings, advertising regularly in the top 30 American market of Charlotte sought to dispel that view. The tag line in every Mart notice announced, "we're worth the trip". Getting its story out in regional newspapers was paramount to waking shoppers up to the fact that quality, selection and discount prices could be found in one location. The narrative went on to say the HFM was an easy drive from Charlotte, where "you'll find the largest furniture manufacturer-related showroom in the Southeast. Located in North Carolina's world-renowned furniture manufacturing country of Hickory, there are 10 acres of fine-quality home and

---

132   "Catawba Visual Art League Sponsors Competition", CO, June 6, 1990, CVN, p. 7.
133   "ASID Chapter Holds Meeting In Hickory", CO, June 20, 1990, CVN, p. 11; "Regional Meeting", CO, June 24, 1990, CVN, p. 31.

office furnishings...over 40 exclusive individual galleries including the industry's most prestigious lines." The number of lines and the acreage of showrooms continued to climb as the months and years advanced. So sure that furniture shoppers would be pleasantly surprised by what awaited them that the Mart offered a rather startling offer. "We're so sure you will be delighted, we'll buy you a tank of gas if you're not satisfied once you've seen everything," was their proposition.[134]

Hickory Furniture Mart advertising did not stand still. Each month brought news of new and/or expanding showrooms. Berkline Comfort Gallery opened "on the third level of the 10 acre home furnishings complex." Headquartered in Morristown, Tennessee, Berkline made "popularly priced upholstery, motion upholstery and reclining chairs."[135] Another new addition demonstrated how important considerations other than furniture were in creating the perfect home or office. Tony Watts "opened the Final Touch, a new gallery featuring lighting and accessories for the home and office at the Hickory Furniture Mart." Watts also owned/operated Gallery of Lights in the HFM.[136]

There was always news of expansion by tenants at the Mart. National Furniture Distributors expanded their footprint by moving up to the terrace level, "accessible from the Mart's new west entrance." The store "sells furniture, art, rugs and accessories."[137] Showrooms vied for the eye of the customer and jockeyed for position to capture the interest of those who walked in the door.

Part of the mission of HFM, beyond sales, was educating the

134	"Hickory Furniture Mart" (advert), CO, July 1, 1990, p. 6A.
135	"Furniture Gallery", CO, August 1, 1990, CVN, p. 13.
136	"Lighting Gallery Opens", CO, August 8, 1990, CVN, p. 19.
137	"Store Moves at Mart", CO, September 26, 1990, CVN, p. 14.

buyer about their purchases. The Furniture Festival had been an effort to instill pride and appreciation for the furniture industry, long part of the local economy. At the Fourth Annual Furniture Festival, students and faculty from CVCC demonstrated "latest in upholstery technology/interior design." Eddie Hamrick crafted furniture on site, using "authentic hand tools reminiscent of 18th century woodworking." A number of other artisans showed visitors the intricacies of their work. Skills like painting, etching, and chair caning were all part of the festival, something of a living history lesson.[138] Mart personnel worked hard to enhance the experience for those who came with regular upgrades of the Catawba Valley Furniture Museum. A new Visitor's Center was also added.[139]

Another way to offer buyers a learning experience was to help them understand the product they were buying. Understanding how a piece was built including the labor and materials that went into it, helped when it came to buying with confidence. The Mart did not want consumers to be baffled by industry jargon. Some of HFM's advertising was much more informational than promotional. One notice explained it as such:

> "Sometimes it's a whole lot easier for the buying public to make sense of what they like than it is for them to understand furniture lingo. Yet an understanding of some of the terminology used within the industry can assist buyers in acquiring the education and know-how necessary to select quality home furnishings of long lasting value. Hickory Furniture Mart

---

[138] "Furniture Festival Saturday", CO, July 25, 1990, p. CVN, p. 10.
[139] "New Visitor's Center at Mart", CO, September 2, 1990. CVN, p. 38.

Design Center offers an alphabetized list of commonly used furniture literature and conversation. In an effort to further educate a buying public increasingly concerned with the value of what they purchase, Hickory Furniture Mart has agreed to let us bring its glossary of furniture terms in this special section."

"Banding: Decorative inlay or marquetry."
"Cabriole: Leg curving outward, descending in tapering reverse curve ending in ornamental foot."
"Case piece: Furniture providing interior storage space."
"Chinoiserie: Lacquered or painted Chinese design"
"Crotch veneer: Veneer cut from branching point of tree, producing interesting   patterns."
"Hand-tied: Method of attaching single coil springs to webbing and frame to achieve elasticity. Two-, four-, and eight-way ties are common, with quality of construction determined by the higher number of ties."
"Knock-off: Industry term referring to obvious copy of popular design, reproduced and sold at a lower price."
"Occasional furniture: Small furniture pieces such as end tables, chests, pull-up chairs; with various uses in a room."
"Stretcher: Crosspieces or bracings under chairs or tables, connecting legs."
"Tight seat: Fully upholstered seat or back, without cushion."
"Tuxedo sofa: Simple upholstered sofa with thin sides, playing

slightly, sides same height as back."

"Wing chair: Large upholstered chair with sides projecting from high back."[140]

This condensed list demonstrates the depths HFM intended to educate customers on what they were buying. Believing that an educated customer will do their homework before buying and therefore be happier with their purchase, the Mart and the stores within it wanted to make sure that another of their mottos rang true, "Quality, Variety, Value. Hickory Furniture Mart. North Carolina's Largest."[141]

As the dominant furniture retail center in the region, Furniture Mart advertising took seriously the task of continuing to educate consumers as well as enticing them. Under the title "Upholstery: What You Don't See Is As Important As What You Do," text included several important pointers to those looking for a well-crafted piece of furniture. The article explained the value of cushioning to comfort and longevity of a chair or sofa, advising that "down is the cushioning material of preference in much high-end upholstered furniture." The primer went on to say that synthetic fillers were also "viable," but cautioned that "whatever the cushioning material, resilience and comfort should be the primary characteristics." The article went on to suggest tips on care and cleaning for any upholstery, giving readers a taste of the help offered at Hickory Furniture Mart.[142]

By the end of the 1980s, the Mart had fully morphed into some-

---

140 "Glossary Helps With Furniture Lingo", CO, September 30, 1990, p. 2Z.
141 "After Market Sale" (advert), CO, October 31, 1990, p. 9A.
142 "Upholstery: What You Don't See Is As Important As What You Do," CO, October 27, 1991, p. 3Z.

thing that High Point could not touch. Instead of a closed market, made for only wholesale buyers, HFM had flung open its doors to everyone. Among the multitudes of showrooms was a story in each of the manufacturers getting closer to the customer. Sometimes the items sold were leftovers from the High Point market. Following the fall market of 1990, Drexel Heritage opened its own "Factory Outlet Store" offering showroom and photography samples, discontinued merchandise and slightly imperfect pieces."[143]

Other tenants were some of the retailers that had just come from High Point. "Hickory Park Furniture Galleries inside the Hickory Furniture Mart has remodeled its Hammary Gallery to show a new line of upholstered furniture introduced by Hammary Furniture Co. at the recent International Furniture Market," read one announcement.[144] The beauty of walking through the Mart was the variety of options shopping there allowed.

While Hickory Furniture Mart was not the only retail outlet for buying furniture, it was the largest. Between Lenoir and Hickory, dozens of individual showrooms offered a few lines from which to choose. However, to see it all meant driving from one to the other, which often proved cumbersome, and took a lot of time and effort. Once folks left their car in the parking lot, they could leave it there for the day. Going from one showroom to another was a process that only took a few steps, not another car ride. And with everything form leftovers to new lines on display, it was like retail buyers were in on the Furniture Market, only in Hickory they were welcomed, not barred from entry. Clearly, HFM had taken the

---

143   "Outlet Store Opens at Mart", CO, October 28, 1990, CVN, p. 10.
144   "Remodeled Hickory Park Gallery Open", CO, January 28, 1991, CVN, p. 15.

idea of a retail buying space and ran with it, much to its own success and the delight of shoppers. North Carolina had become 'the place' to buy furniture, near where it was made. "Although the High Point market is closed to the public, shoppers at Hickory Furniture Mart can still benefit from this major international event. Many Mart stores sell furniture and accessories straight off the Market's showroom floor."[145]

It no longer mattered that the twice annual Furniture Market had moved. Hickory's reputation as a center for furniture remained intact because the transformation of Hickory Furniture Mart into retail space meant a continuation of furniture buying in Hickory, only spread over the year. There was, however, an emphasis on the excitement the market brought, even if it was 150 miles away. "Hickory Furniture Mart's semi-annual After Market Sales are eagerly awaited by thousands of informed buyers who have found there is no better time or place to buy the best furniture at the best prices." With each After Market Sale, numbers increased as advertising, but also word of mouth ensured popularity.[146]

With its own Visitor's Center and furniture museum, HFM had been its own welcome center. So it was not a surprise when managers of the public welcome centers came calling. In 1991, Hickory Furniture Mart hosted a "private treasure hunt" as part of "the N.C. Welcome Center Familiarization Tour for managers of welcome centers touring the area." Clues were given to the managers who roamed the store looking for answers "John Schenk and Brad Lail, President and Vice President of Hickory Furniture Mart," conducted the event, proving once again the popularity of the site.[147]

---

145   "North Carolina is World's Largest Furniture Market" CO. April 28, 1991, p. 2Y.
146   "It's Smart To Shop After Market Sales", CO, April 28, 1991, p. 1Y.
147   "Welcome center managers go on private treasure hunt", CO, April 21, 1991, CVN, p.

The recognition of the Mart as a draw for tourists (and furniture shoppers) to Hickory had been established. For any artist to have such a facility to showcase their work was a great boon. So when Conover artist Vae Hamilton was offered a one-woman show, it was quite a prestigious event. The announcement revealed that "Hamilton, best known for contemporary Southwestern paintings, will have 14 paintings on display and for sale. She will be working during the show on two large portraits using water and acrylic paints."[148]

In May of 1991, another sign of the Mart's expansion came at the expense of its next door neighbor, Mull's Restaurant. A component of the Mull's complex since the Mart opened in 1960, the restaurant had been the "unofficial headquarters for furniture execs" as well as shoppers who came in for refreshment after the market left town. However, Mull's became a casualty of the Mart's growth. It closed to make room for the expansion of the Mart. The original Hickory Furniture Mart began its life underneath Mull's Restaurant but now, after many additions, the property became incredibly valuable for retail furniture sales, and less so for food.[149]

With the closing of Mull's Restaurant came the announcement of expansion for the Hickory Furniture Mart. Acknowledged as already "the largest public home furnishings display in North Carolina, the notice revealed that another 70,000 square feet "of new showroom space" was coming soon. The "four-story addition" was slated for the south side of the complex.[150]

16.
148   "One-woman show", CO, March 29, 1991, CVN, p. 14.
149   Carol D. Leonnig, "Closing strands breakfast gang", CO, May 24, 1991, CVN, p. 1,3.
150   "What's New", CO, May 27, 1991, p. 5D

Before there was even a brick laid in the expansion, retailers inside were continuing to fill up the available square footage. Franklin Place announced it was expanding, adding a "large lower level space to its showroom on the building's upper level."[151]

It wasn't just business that was going on. The Hickory Furniture Mart had become part of the fabric of the Catawba Valley. During FreedomFest, a five day celebration of the July 4th holiday, the Mart was one of numerous places where events, mostly sporting, took place. Bike races, crafts, and fireworks were all part of the activities and along with Lenoir-Rhyne College, downtown Hickory and Valley Hills Mall, the Mart hosted events. The Mart itself featured tethered hot air balloon rides all day on July 5th.[152]

Meanwhile, the Mart continued to increase business. Advertisements offered a 1-800 number to call for information about hours, driving directions and a rundown of the "over 40 exclusive individual galleries." There was much to come and see. "There are many exciting activities, a Visitor's Center and a Furniture Museum too," offered an ad, asserting "everything your heart desires for your home is right here - at affordable prices."[153]

The Mart now served as a mecca for retail furniture, in much the same way it had for manufacturers, only this time the attraction was year-round. In 1991, Mart officials quantified the draw. Over 200,000 shoppers were coming each year to see the selection of furniture from a myriad of dealers. Each time they came there was more to see with addi-

---

151   "What's New", CO. June 3, 1991, p. 7D.
152   "Coming Soon", CO, June 14, 1991, CVN, p. 4; "Schedule of Events" CO, June 23, 1991, Iredell Neighbors, p. 10Z; "Hickory Furniture Mart", CO, June 21, 1991, CVN, p. 10.
153   "Hickory Furniture Mart" (advert), CO, June 23, 1991, Iredell Neighbors, p. 5Z.

tions coming online regularly. Those consumers looking to furnish their homes were generating "some $26 million for the area's hospitality industry," an amount that surpassed the days of the old Furniture Market.[154]

Not only was the Mart a location for shopping, it was also a center for meeting planning. "The Carolinas Chapter of Meeting Planners International" held a reception at the Hickory Furniture Mart, with breakout meetings around town. The organization, with a number of local members in attendance, used the courtyard for their gathering of 65. The multipurpose nature of Mart space was growing.[155]

The idea of Hickory adding to its allure as a meeting site prompted HFM to band together with Clement Center, the Holiday Inn Piedmont Center, Hampton Inn and Holiday Inn Express to form Hickory Host, Inc. The purpose of the group was "to increase tourism and bring regional meetings to the Unifour" which included Catawba, Burke, Caldwell and Alexander counties. The new organization planned to more successfully compete with North Carolina cities like Charlotte, Asheville and Fayetteville.[156]

The plan began to work. Before 1991 was over, the N.C. Travel Council hosted its annual convention in town. Thanks in large part to Brad Lail who "was instrumental in bringing the meeting to Hickory," the convention of some 160 toured Century Furniture, a timely reminder of Hickory's furniture presence.[157] When the N.C. Association of District Court Judges and the N.C. Conference of Chief District Court Judges held

---

154   "Shop to add Bernhardt line at mart", CO, June 26, 1991, CVN, p. 10.
155   "Meeting planners gather", CO, July 17, 1991, CVN, p. 8.
156   "New Hickory Host group working to increase tourism", CO, August 25, 1991, CVN, p. 18.
157   "Travel Council meets here", CO, November 3, 1991, CVN, p. 12.

their fall conference in Hickory, a reception was given at the Mart.[158] Conventions including the N.C. Association of Festivals, all made stops at the Mart during their time in Hickory.[159]

Soon, the Hickory Furniture Mart featured items made all from over the world. "Stix, Corp., distributor of imported furnishings opened a factory store on the lower level" that included a variety of "chairs, chests, tables barstools, love seats and dining room tables," expanding further the choices for shoppers coming to Hickory to buy their furniture.[160]

Though furniture from great distances now served to attract consumers to Hickory, the local furniture industry, which in essence served as the reason the Hickory Furniture Mart began in the first place, remained the heart of the Mart's identity. Leroy Lail recognized that many people coming to town were looking for furniture. Estimates were that eight out of ten visitors "ask about furniture or furniture-shopping," according to a survey by the Catawba County Chamber of Commerce. Lail's answer was to beef up the Visitor's Center in the Mart, to help guide those visitors. And while the Visitor's Center aided many a shopper, it did not capture the imagination, nor answer questions in the same way his next creation did.[161]

Asserting that spokesperson icons like Smoky the Bear, Morris the Cat, and the Pillsbury Doughboy all took on a life of their own as the persona of the entities they represented (the U.S. Forest Service, Nine Lives cat food, and the pastry maker, respectively),western North Caroli-

---

158   Louise Barrett, "District judges hold meeting here", CO, November 6, 1991, CVN, p. 3.
159   "Festival Folks Gather", CO, November 13, 1991, CVN, p. 8
160   "Stix factory store", CO, October 21, 1991, CVN, p. 13.
161   "Hickory Furniture Mart Vistor's Center Offers Information, Free Maps, Brochures", CO, October 27, 1991, p. 2Z.

na furniture needed its own embodiment. He called the new character "Abel," a figure "forged in the mold of a late-1800's furniture crafter." Seeking to make furniture buying fun, as well as easy and economical, Abel offered assistance and education to those coming to town. "We have long felt a need for some sort of symbol that could bring into focus the furniture pride that pervades the Catawba Valley area," said Lail about the new public face of furniture. "We hope Abel will become that symbol."[162]

Recognizing in 1991 that the rich history of the industry was being lost in the upheaval that shifted the wholesale market from Hickory and the emergent retail market that the Mart cultivated, Lail argued that in the questions visitors had about where to buy, they also were interested in the precedents that brought them to the Catawba Valley. "It seems," he said, "Hickory Furniture Mart has become the keeper of the history and heritage and pride of the Catawba Valley furniture industry." He believed that "creating the character of Abel is another step toward preserving furniture pride and history," adding "we've created this character from the late 19th century because that is the period in which North Carolina moved to the forefront of the furniture industry in this country."[163]

For Leroy Lail, education spurred interest, interest spurred sales. At times, the savings offered were substantial. In one advertisement the headline read, "Furnish Yourself With Up To 80% Savings." With names like Drexel Heritage, Henredon and the Ralph Lauren Furniture Collection on the list, the Mart defined itself as "the largest manufacturer-owned clearance center in the United States."[164]

The Furniture Mart opened its doors to a wide range of public

---

162 "'Abel' is Mart's Answer to Furniture Questions", CO, October 27, 1991, p. 2Z.
163 "'Abel' is Mart's Answer to Furniture Questions", CO, October 27, 1991, p. 2Z.
164 "Furnish Yourself With Up To 80% Savings", CO, November 10, 1991, p. 12A.

service events too. "Kids in Concert Suzuki students" made a stop during the Christmas season. A reception was held for the Western Piedmont Symphony who welcomed the Lettermen to a Mother's Day event.[165] The Mart also sponsored a wide array of demonstrations. In the courtyard, "Sandy Adair of Fibre Designs" demonstrated the art of tapestry weaving. [166]

The Mart had become a tourist destination that equaled many other attractions around the state. In one newspaper supplement, Brevard offered its waterfalls, Grandfather Mountain its vistas, Greensboro its Revolutionary War history and its golf tournament, but in Hickory the place to be was the Furniture Mart. Heralding its variety, its size and convenience, the Mart had become a showplace for furniture buying, with images of its four-story west entrance to demonstrate the grandeur. In fact, the Raleigh News and Observer ranked the top ten brochures in the state with Hickory Furniture Mart placing right up there with Carowinds, and the North Carolina Zoo.[167] A survey by the North Carolina Department of Travel and Tourism proved it. Seeking to find the twenty most "well-known attractions" in the state, the Mart's popularity rivaled that of Old Salem, Discovery Place in Charlotte, and Tweetsie as a destination.[168]

It seemed everyone coming to Hickory was making a stop at the Mart, including former Soviets. Boris Yusfin, a Russian bank president said, "we find in your city kind relationships and a most kind welcome.

---

165   Louise Barrett, "Students to take bows amid boughs:, CO, November 22, 1991, CVN, p. 6; "Lettermen, symphony to perform together at Mother's Day event", CO, April 24, 1992, CVN, p. 6.
166   Louise Barrett, "Tapestry weaving exhibit", CO, February 21, 1992, CVN, p. 5.
167   "For Furniture…It's Hickory Furniture Mart", CO, March 29, 1992, (North Carolina Vacation Guide), p. 2; "Send For Free Travel Brochures", News & Observer (Raleigh), March 29, 1992, (North Carolina Vacation Guide), p. 7.
168   "Mart Among Top N.C. Attractions" CO, April 26, 1992, (Furniture Preview Section), p. 12Z.

We've found we haven't seen anything like that before," Yusfin, with a contingent of businessmen from Russia, toured the Hickory Furniture Mart. Yusfin added, "It's so impressive." Six years later, when a group of furniture makers from Russia came to the United States, they also visited the Mart to see business at the retail level. The nine men and one woman from "the Russian cities of Yekaterinburg, Rostov-on-Don and Volgograd" were anxious to see the American process. They spent three weeks in North Carolina visiting mostly factories, but HFM was a unique stop on their tour.[169]

The prominent contingent of Russian leaders was not even the highest profile visitor from the old Soviet Union to the Mart. Kateryna Yushchenko, wife of then Ukrainian President Viktor Yushchenko, shopped at Hickory Furniture Mart during a visit to the United States. Her purchase of home furnishings was one of the largest for a single customer at stores within the Mart.[170]

There have been a lot of celebrities that have bought furniture at HFM, either personally or through someone outfitting their home. A number of NASCAR drivers, NFL players, and professional golfers have shopped at the Mart. Several times Hickory Furniture Mart has been highlighted on national television, most notably on the Oprah Winfrey Show when Kate Gladchun talked about her experience of buying whole rooms of furniture from various stores in the Mart. HFM even turned up in a humorous comparison piece with IKEA where Stephen Colbert (himself a South Carolina native) tried to sit on an IKEA made item, which

---

169 Shirley Hunter Moore, "Charm impresses former Soviets", CO, April 5, 1992, CVN, p. 1, 17; Pete Prunkl, "Russian furniture execs brave language barriers", CO, February 8, 1998, p. 6V.
170 Interview with Brad Lail, Tracey Trimble, Hickory Furniture Mart, August 27, 2020.

came apart, then on a Hickory Chair piece, demonstrating the durability of furniture that came from the Mart. When the Carolina Panthers were in Super Bowl 50 against the Denver Broncos, pre-game coverage included a look at what made the Charlotte region unique. The segment included Hickory Furniture Mart.[171] HFM Vice President and Chief Financial Officer Scott Lail welcomed the attention, especially in the early days of the conversion of the Mart to retail. "We were so hungry, having lost the wholesale showroom and going back in retail. I think we were really happy to have the attention." It signified that the Lail family had made the right decision to transition to a new clientele, instead of throwing in the towel as some did in Hickory after the loss of the Southern Furniture Market. For Hickory and HFM, its best days were still ahead.[172]

Meanwhile, more lines continued to seek space in the Mart. Clayton Marcus, Highland House, all housed showcases at the Mart.[173] All the while, the Mart continued to grow. By the summer of 1992, stores within totaled 60 and the acreage covered in furniture had grown to twelve.[174]

Every inch of space was subject to renovation and repurposing. The old Mull's Convention Center became a "new home for old treasures" as the "Antique Center at the Mart" opened in the fall of 1992. Populated by dealers showing and selling "high-middle to high-end range" antiques, the Mart found yet another way to attract home owners looking for unusual items for their decor.[175]

By that point, an entirely new wing had opened. Offering an

---

171   Interview with Brad Lail, Tracey Trimble, Hickory Furniture Mart, August 27, 2020.
172   Interview with Scott Lail, Hickory Furniture Mart, September 2, 2020.
173   "Clayton Marcus Showcase" CO, May 13, 1992, CVN, p. 5; "New galleries", CO, May 24, 1992, CVN, p. 6.
174   "Hickory Furniture Mart (advert), CO, September 2, 1992, p. 11A.
175   "New home for old treasures", CO, September 13, 1992, CVN, p. 6.

additional 70,000 square-feet, the Mart had grown to "more than a half million square feet of showrooms under one roof." In that space, buyers could now shop for lines from Frederick Edward, Maitland-Smith, Marbo, Smith & Gains, and Universal.[176]

Every possible variation of furnishings for the home could be found at Hickory Furniture Mart. "Generations by Hickory Park," a line of children's furniture added to the wide array of choices for the growing number of shoppers, who asked for "a place to buy furnishings and accessories for children's rooms."[177] "Hickory Home Outfitters - newly opened, this four-story south addition of the Hickory Furniture Mart brings together in one wing 20 true factory outlets," read another announcement.[178]

The idea was to keep folks comfortable while they shopped. Shoppers get hungry and to that end, the Mart enhanced its food offering so customers would not have to prowl around town for lunch. Jane Moore, who started Jessica's Cafe in the Mart as a eatery, expanded both space and offerings as Jessica's Porch. The new incarnation opened in 1992.[179]

As Mart operations progressed, a number of improvements were taking place. Catawba County Historical Association's Sidney Halma provided his assistance to take the furniture museum, located on the first floor of the Mart, to a new level. Leroy Lail, who had moved up to the position of Chairman of the Board of the Mart, said, "We're updating the museum to more accurately represent the development of furniture making in the Catawba Valley area and to add excitement to the exhibits."

---

176   "Major Mart Addition Introduces Unique Concept", CO, October 25, 1992, p. 1Z.
177   "Complete Children's Gallery Open at Hickory Furniture Mart", October 25, 1992, p. 7Z.
178   CO, October 25, 1992, (Special Advertising Section), p. 8Z.
179   "What's New", CO, October 26, 1992, p. 7D.

Lenoir-Rhyne College theatre professor Ray Mills designed the upgrade. Among the new exhibits was a "representation of a woodworking shop at a family farm in Catfish (northeastern Catawba County). Lail added, "The furniture mill replica will be the starting point of a self-directed tour of the Furniture Museum." From there, visitors could see the progression of furniture making, much of it crafted in nearby factories. The latest editions of chairs, sofas and chests, grandchildren of the historical pieces, were available for visitors to purchase at the Mart's stores.[180]

Upon completion of the new furniture history museum came the need to document the companies that were part of the growth of the industry in the twentieth century. A "furniture family tree" became necessary to determine the myriad of companies that began to produce furniture, some later consolidating into larger operations. As chairman of HFM, Leroy Lail put out a call for the community to help identify the names of companies that were part of the phenomenal growth of the industry in the western portion of state, the "furniture figure-eight." The western circle encompassed Hickory, Morganton, Marion and Lenoir was the primary focus of the family tree. He left the Mart's number for contributors to call.[181]

Along with marriages and art shows, perhaps one of the most unique events to be hosted at the Mart was "the Catawba County Chamber of Commerce's annual Business Spelling Bee," part of a "Business After Hours" function. The idea was to raise money for the Chamber's educational programs. Businesses could sponsor a team of four, presumably their best spellers.[182]

---

180   "History gets new look at furniture museum", CO, December 13, 1992, CVN, p. 14.
181   "Furniture Family Tree", CO, July 17, 1994, CVN, p. 5.
182   "Chamber to hold spelling bee on Dec. 14. at furniture mart", November 10, 1996, p.

Like the spelling bee, the Mart constantly offered free events to the entire community as a way to not only attract customers but also to showcase the rich offering of talent in the Catawba Valley. "Art in the Mart" served as a continuing example for painters in "acrylics, oils, landscapes, florals, still lives, watercolors and other works of art." Artists from Statesville to Lenoir set up easels for display of their work in the courtyard.[183]

The venue became such a premier site for displaying art that the Hickory Museum of Art kicked off its own exhibit of 19th century works by American artists with a display and reception. The works came from "one of the country's most important private art collections" and featured paintings that were previously on display "at the National Gallery of Art in Washington and the Museum of Art in New York." The exhibit, "Through Artists' Eyes: 19th Century America" featured "the works of the best known and lesser known artists of their respective periods."[184]

Music too, became an important offering of the Mart. Hickory's "Sweet Adelines," a group of about 20 women specializing in barbershop harmony" filled the atrium as part of the "Music at the Mart" series. Jessica's Porch restaurant served free apple cider and a gingerbread house "prepared by award-winning chefs at Hickory's Holiday Inn Piedmont Center" was displayed in the courtyard during the concert.[185]

One important tenant was also one of the largest advertisers within the Mart, DonLamor, Inc. With a regular newspaper presence, the retailer offered furniture at 30 to 45% off suggested retail and included

---
4V.
183   "Art In The Mart", CO, January 29, 1993, CVN, p. 1.
184   "Hickory art museum displays 19th century American works", Asheville Citizen-Times, March 7, 1993, p. 3L.
185   "Mart Music", CO, December 17, 1993, CVN, p. 1.

brands such as Vanguard, Pennsylvania House, National Mount Airy, Classic Leather and Statesville Chair. "Service is priority #1" was the motto at DonLamor and during the "After Market Sale" shoppers could find items for "up to 75% off retail." But they did want customers to "come early."[186]

Christmas became especially festive at the Mart. Holiday performances from area musicians filled the atrium with song as the a number of performers sang and played yuletide favorites for visitors. Some came just to hear the music. Others enjoyed the mood as they shopped. Pianist Pat Geese played, while Kids In Koncert sang carols to ring in the season.[187]

It didn't take long for Hickory Furniture Mart to become enough of a significant entity to find its presence in other shows. The annual Southern Spring Show in Charlotte saw the Mart "furnish and decorate one of 21 designer rooms to be included in the 1993 edition of the South's premier flower, garden, indoor and outdoor living exposition." The Mart's contribution was a "European villa theme," with "all furniture and accessories" coming from the stores and galleries of the Hickory Furniture Mart. When it returned for a second year at the Spring Show with a room called "Carolina Retreat", the Mart was honored for the contribution.[188]

The third year proved to be the charm at the Southern Spring Show, This time Mart creations placed in three of four categories, winning first prize for the Designer House South's master bedroom display. "We were absolutely thrilled with what Hickory Furniture Mart did,"

---

186   "DonLamor, Inc.", CO, October 30, 1992, CVN, p. 7.
187   "Music at the mart", CO, December 11, 1992, CVN, p. 5.
188   "Spring Show will feature designer room by Hickory Furniture Mart", CO, February 5, 1993, CVN, p. 2; "Display honored", CO, March 9, 1994, CVN, p. 5V.

commented Joan Zimmerman, Founder and President of the Southern Spring Show. Calling the Mart's effort "overwhelming," she went on to say that "the judges were particularly impressed with the absolute and complete attention to detail."[189]

By 1993, Hickory Furniture Mart had become a landmark in Catawba County. When conventions came to town, the Mart was a stop on every list. The Greater Hickory Convention and Visitor's Bureau organized events for conventioneers, like the 1993 Association of Fire Chiefs and Association of Fire Fighters convention. Along with a tour of the Mart, the fire fighters were treated to a golf tournament as well as visits to the other historic sites in the area.[190]

Hickory Furniture Mart became a substantial reason for visitors to come to Hickory. It also sought to accommodate those who came by remaining attuned to their needs. In a message from Mart management, called "You Ask And We Deliver," a number of improvements were cited that came from visitor requests. When furniture buyers said they needed more choice, the Mart expanded its showrooms, when some asked about where to buy antiques to accessorize their newly bought suites, an "Antique Center at the Mart" opened. Patrons who wanted to make the trip a two-day affair needed hotel space close to the Mart, so a Holiday Inn Express opened "just across the parking lot." The Mart kept tabs on the "wish list" shoppers supplied, showing a responsiveness not seen in many other places.[191]

Throughout its tenure as a retail outlet, the Mart remained an im-

---

189   "Furniture Mart Wins", CO, March 17, 1995, p. 4V.
190   "Hickory to host fire chiefs, firefighters", CO, February 21, 1993, CVN, p. 8.
191   "You Ask And We Deliver: A Message From Mart Management", CO, April 25, 1993, p. 11Z.

portant setting for visual artists to display their work. Often that included photographers as well. The Catawba Valley Visual Arts League held their Annual Spring Art Competition at Hickory Furniture Mart with their submissions on display there. The contest awarded 19 prizes to members with the Mart showcasing their work. The artists also gained an audience from shoppers coming for furniture that occasionally walked away with the artists' pieces to adorn their walls as well.[192]

By 1993, the Mart had grown into a mammoth enterprise. Now with twelve acres of space for "factory stores, outlets and galleries" which totaled more than 65, it attracted "more than 300,000 visitors annually." The most crowded time for the Mart was generally its After Market Sales but given the array of promotions and events held there on a weekly basis, the doors of the Mart were always swinging during its operating hours of 9am to 6pm weekdays, and 9-5 on Saturdays. They even opened on Sundays, occasionally.[193]

The 1990s proved there was no looking back to the days of the Furniture Market in Hickory for the Mart. The conversion to a retail outlet caused the building to expand almost annually. The annual Furniture Festival, held every summer, had grown to such proportions that a waiting list for prospective exhibitors had to be kept. Among the attractions to the seventh-annual event was a "$1,000 Shopping Spree" giveaway, sponsored by the Charlotte Observer.[194]

The experience of working in such a dynamic and engaging venue as the Hickory Furniture Mart provided experience that other organi-

---
192 "Spring Art Competition", CO, May 7, 1993, CVN, p. 6.
193 "After Market Sale a success", CO, May 9, 1993, CVN, p. 15; "Mart sets special hours", CO, August 29, 1993, CVN, p. 17.
194 "Furniture Festival to Expand", CO, July 7, 1993, CVN, p. 4; "Win A $1000 Shopping Spree" (advert), CO, July 18, 1993, p. 6C.

zations wanted to hear about. One example was Tracey Bolick, Marketing Director for the Mart. At the quarterly meeting of the North Carolina Council of Shopping Centers, she was the guest speaker. Bolick gave the council a full recounting of how the Mart became a star attraction in western North Carolina. She also offered a few tips on how HFM maintained that position.[195]

Even with the expansion, the Mart made the point that there was more furniture at outlet prices than even it could hold. "Don't Miss The Big Tent Sale" screamed the banner in advertisements that promised Drexel Heritage, Palliser, Marbro, Thomas Markham, Southern and many more at up to 70% off. The Mart claimed it was "as low as we go." It had gone so low, the merchandise now had to exit the building for sale outside.[196]

The dizzying growth and sales at the Hickory Furniture Mart never caused anyone involved to shelf the past with its prelude to what made such activity possible. During Furniture History Month in October of 1993, the Mart took a day to "pay tribute to its owners, Leroy and Lynn Mull Lail, for their 30 years with the company and their continuing efforts to preserve the history and heritage of the furniture industry in the Catawba Valley." An event called "Remember Hickory Reunion" recounted the path from the Mart's first days to its current, under the guiding hand of the Lail's, whose vision and hard work had paid off in substantial ways.[197]

The Mart itself now held a place in the history of the furniture industry in the South. Its transformation had been a study in adaptabil-

---

195   "Council of Shopping Centers", CO, August 8, 1993, CVN, p. 6.
196   "For 3 Days This Is As Low As We Go", CO, September 26, 1993, Iredell Neighbors, p. 9I.
197   "Furniture History Month", CO, October 3, 1993, CVN, p. 4V.

ity. Furniture production had always been in flux, from the time finely crafted pieces were created by artisans in Boston prior to the American Revolution. After following the forests of the west, production came down south and mechanized after the Civil War. For over a century it became a mainstay of the economy in North Carolina. By the 1990s, change was afoot again. Industry analysts feared the move of manufacturers offshore. Hickory Furniture Mart, through the ingenuity and perseverance of the Lails, had weathered change within the industry. Actually, that change had been good for Hickory in many ways, evening out the flood of visitors from two times per year to a regular, daily trek of customers coming for near-wholesale prices in a retail environment. Hickory had the Lails to thank for keeping it synonymous with furniture manufacturing long after the Southern Furniture Market had left town.[198]

When a listing of "heritage spots" was printed for tourists, Hickory Furniture Mart was listed as a stop in Catawba County, along with the Catawba Science Center and the Hickory Museum of Art. The listing demonstrated just how important HFM was to the economic life of the region. While some counties featured their historic sites, Catawba offered commerce as a part of its attractions.[199]

The complex at the Mart continued to grow right along with the Mart itself. Adding diversity and amenities that furniture shoppers sought, Shoppes at the Mart opened a plethora of small operations with a variety of services. Among the first was the Scarlet Butterfly in 1987, a women's clothing store. Alma Dixon Kincaid followed that with the open-

---

198 "Hickory Furniture Mart Hold Honored Position In History of Industry", CO, October 24, 1993, p. 6Z.
199 Audrey Y. Williams, "Trips back in time", CO, July 27, 1997, p. 1, 10L.

ing of the Cutting Edge, a hairstyling business.[200]

No sooner had 1994 arrived than news came too of another expansion of the Hickory Furniture Mart. In January Mart officials revealed the addition of "a four-story expansion that will make its building one of the largest public furniture centers on the East Coast." The new part added another 70,000 square feet, doubling the size of the wing. According to Mart President John Schenk there were other building projects in the works with plans to eventually expand Mart offerings by "at least 190,000 square feet. In addition, another road to allow customers a secondary access point to the Mart hit the drawing board with a 1.3 mile road paralleling Highway 70 behind the Mart and its neighbor, Valley Hills Mall as an alternative entrance. "We're expanding to accommodate demand both from existing tenants and from people who have been waiting for a change to get new lines into the building," said Schenk. Soon, the Hickory Furniture Mart began billing itself as "North Carolina's Largest." And it was.[201] Before year's end, the new space filled up. Among those seeking space was Virginia House, owned by Herb Greene, who installed a gallery.[202]

Continuing to be a good community partner, when the need arose to refurbish the dining room of Sipe's Orchard Home, numerous companies within the Mart as well as the Mart itself donated to the cause. Sipe's Orchard Home was a facility started "in 1943 to provide care for neglected, abused and homeless boys." Its campus, in nearby Conover began as

---

200 "Hairstyling Business Opens", CO, December 15, 1993, CVN, p. 6V; Beverly Brown, "Hickory Furniture Design Center Gets New Tenants", CO, December 27, 1987, CVN, p. 14.
201 "Furniture company expands", Asheville Citizen-Times, January 8, 1994, p. 5B; Shirley Hunter Moore, "Hickory Furniture Mart to sprout more space, road", CO, January 28, 1994, CVN, p. 1V; CO, February 12, 1994, p. 11A.
202 "Virginia House new at Mart", CO, November 29, 1994, p. 10V.

a working farm, over the years transitioning its site for therapy. What V.O. and Viola Sipe began as a place to prepare "children and youth for their best futures" quickly became a community supported effort. The dining room soon had the flare of a Hickory Furniture Mart showroom.[203]

The Mart remained attuned to the needs of the Hickory area. Following the 1994 Furniture Festival, the Mart presented a check for $3,000 to Habitat For Humanity. Vice President Brad Lail presented the donation "as a tribute to the Catawba Valley furniture industry and the people who make this a national furniture center." To help the local Hospice organization, the Women's League of Hickory and the Hickory Junior Woman's Club partnered with the Hickory Furniture Mart to host an auction to raise money. A number of popular items of memorabilia including autographed items from Michael Jordan and Dale Earnhardt were "available during the live auction."[204]

During the AIDS crisis, the Lail's offered the Mart for fundraising to ALFA, the AIDS Leadership Foothills-Area Alliance, centered in Hickory. As part of several "dinner parties across town," Leroy and Lynn Lail "donated use of their 13 acre main building," for the kickoff event.[205]

Hickory Furniture Mart had bred a new type of retail customer, the "power shopper." Inspired by Kate Gladchun who wrote the book on the subject, called "The Fine Furniture and Furnishings Discount Shopping Guide," the Mart attracted customers to Hickory with one goal in mind. Buy. Gladchun led a group of women from their homes in Michigan, the state where the furniture industry was based in the 19th century

---

203   https://www.sipesorchardhome.org/story/
204   CO, October 30, 1994, p. 7Z; "Make Your Bid", CO, November 11, 1994, p. 1V.
205   Monte Mitchell, "AIDS dinner fund-raisers ready for takeoff in Unifour", CO, May 12, 1995, p. 1-6V.

before being usurped by the South, to Hickory. When they got to town their rallying cry was "good luck, good deals, good shopping."[206]

New York Times reporters Jane and Michael Stern followed the women to town to see what all the commotion was about. Their reporting revealed just how much power these shoppers had. One member of Gladchun's crew came with $50,000 to furnish her new home entirely. "We are going completely contemporary," she said. Her list of items was long. "I need a living room, a dining room, light fixtures, bathroom fixtures, switch plates, a guest room suite, and '50s furniture for the basement to match the gas pump and Coke machine we already have."[207]

Ideally, the group committed to looking for the needs of each other but as the Sterns reported, the frenzy of buying quickly dissolved unity. Another member of "the girls" (as Gladchun called her group) was caught muttering, "gotta buy it, gotta buy it, gotta buy it." The adage of the members was 'never buy retail,' and at the Mart, they didn't have to. The building was filled with bargains awaiting discovery.[208]

To demonstrate the fervor with which the power shopper came to town, one customer stepped back to look at a piece, trying to decide if it would be right for her home. Not looking where she was going, she dropped "off a loading platform and plummeted 6 feet to the ground." However, it didn't stop her. Following the mantra (they had a lot of them) to shop "till she dropped, then get up and shop some more," she returned to her feet before help could arrive, "dusted off her Bermuda shorts and made her way back upstairs to continue contemplating the big purchase. It didn't take long for her to whip out a credit card. Her companions

---

206 Jane and Michael Stern, "Power Shoppers Invade", CO, Jun 10, 1994, p. 1-2V.
207 Jane and Michael Stern, "Power Shoppers Invade", CO, Jun 10, 1994, p. 1-2V.
208 Jane and Michael Stern, "Power Shoppers Invade", CO, Jun 10, 1994, p. 1-2V.

cheered her on with "go, girl go!" "Falling can't stop me," she said.[209]

These buyers exemplified the type of visitors coming to Hickory Furniture Mart. They knew the reputation of the Mart offering discounted prices and were ready buy it and get it shipped home. It was a thin line the Mart had to walk in offering such prices. According to Tracey Bolick, "we don't want retail stores around the country to rise up and strangle manufacturers." She added, "We have to be sensitive about how we attract customers."[210]

But attracting customers the Mart did, so much so that it brought a team from the New York Times to see what was going on. In their article, the Sterns followed one of Kate Gladchun's groups around and confirmed that "sixty percent of all of America's furniture (as of 1994) is manufactured within 200 miles of Hickory." They also pointed out that the atmosphere of the Mart did not match what most people thought they would have to endure to get a bargain. "Most stores in the Mart consist of elegant showrooms with scrupulously designed vignettes to show off the goods," they reported, a far cry from "an exasperating job-lot discounter at which you suffer rude service and stockroom displays to get the lowest prices." The local workers were even lauded for their "experienced advice," the result of hailing "from generations of local furniture families," who "have known the business all their lives."[211]

The Mart had become a gold mine for the nation's retail furniture (though not paying retail) buyer. The mania got so intense that one of the Michigan buyers got a call from her husband. The bank had alerted him that his card might have been stolen, given all the activity they

---

209   Jane and Michael Stern, "Power Shoppers Invade", CO, Jun 10, 1994, p. 1-2V.
210   Jane and Michael Stern, "Power Shoppers Invade", CO, Jun 10, 1994, p. 1-2V.
211   Jane and Michael Stern, "Power Shoppers Invade", CO, Jun 10, 1994, p. 1-2V.

were seeing with it out of state. She assured him that nothing like that had occurred. It was she that made every single purchase. But the bank remained wary saying that "only someone with a stolen card" spends like that.[212]

The New York Times article was great confirmation of the Mart's reputation, but locals already knew what was going on. Called "the granddaddy of retail malls," Chairman of the Tourist Development Authority, Phil Yount said "the no. 1 reason (tourists) come is for furniture." Hickory City Council member Bruce Meisner echoed Yount's sentiment saying "our major attraction isn't service-oriented, it's retail." Any map of Hickory contained a mark on Highway 70 that showed where the Hickory Furniture Mart was located.[213]

The process of shopping for furniture had gotten so immense, thanks largely to the selection, that the Mart published "Shopping Tips" for folks planning a visit. In the list, they suggesting allowing enough time to shop, asking receptionists and staff designers for help and advice, and making notes as shoppers browsed. The notes, they believed were good reference tools to review, especially during rest breaks. Lastly, but perhaps most importantly, the Mart suggested 'kicking the tires,' so to speak. "Sit on chairs and sofas" along with "test drawers and doors" were the best way to make sure buyers got needed value for their purchases.[214]

The coterie of consumers from Michigan were not an isolated incident. In the fall of 1998, a plane load of 186 shoppers took off in Indianapolis bound for Hickory. They had come for furniture bargains and

---
212   Jane and Michael Stern, "Power Shoppers Invade", CO, Jun 10, 1994, p. 1-2V.
213   Norman Gomlak, "Visitors to Hickory area 'marvel at what they see'", CO, June 17, 1994, p. 1-2V.
214   "Shopping Tips", CO, October 30, 1994, p. 10Z.

with the added incentive of the After Market Sale, they got them.[215]

Kate Gladchun's discovery of Hickory Furniture Mart proved to be a milestone for both her and the Mart. It all began for her when her husband said, "if you have to pay retail, you don't need it." Originally, Gladchun was a math and science major from Michigan. But her grandfather's ties to the Michigan furniture industry and her mother's "flair for decorating" pushed her to get an advanced degree at Michigan State in interior design. From there, she "dabbled in design" but had a greater passion for finding deals. Her first book, "The Fine Furniture and Furnishings Discount Shopping Guide" came about after her husband came home from work one day and said, "you won't believe how many places there are in North Carolina that sell amazing furniture at discount prices. I think I could put together a little booklet of them and actually tell people all about it." With the idea for the book in hand, the couple financed its publication, printing about 5,000 copies.[216]

The only problem was Hickory Furniture Mart wasn't in it. A copy of the first edition reached Tracey Bolick at the Mart, who promptly called Kate Gladchun to ask why. The author said she did not know about Hickory Furniture Mart, which prompted Bolick to reply, "Well, I would like to invite you to come and visit us and see for yourself what we have here. We are the largest place in North Carolina that sells furniture at discount prices."[217]

The Gladchun's planned a flight to North Carolina to see all the furniture offerings of the Tarheel state. When they arrived at Hickory Fur-

---

215 Jennifer Rothacker, "Stuff to sit, lie, dine on sells fast", CO, November 15, 1998, p. 1, 15V.
216 Email from Kate Gladchun to author, September 9, 2020.
217 Email from Kate Gladchun to author, September 9, 2020.

niture Mart, Kate Gladchun described it as follows: "Mind blown! Amazingly nice people. BIG facility. Many different showrooms. Outlets and regular showrooms. We were not really in a buying mode, but in research mode. And I was so so so surprised at the availability of furniture, all types of brands, all price points, brand new and floor samples. I absolutely added Hickory Furniture Mart to my next three editions of the book."[218]

Exposure from the book sent both Kate Gladchun and Hickory Furniture Mart into the stratosphere. Marketing her book to media outlets across the country, her work gained the attention of local television stations, newspapers, radio and magazines. After the New York Times article, came a call from Chicago. A producer from the Oprah Winfrey Show wanted to know about the book and who was the expert on furniture buying. After she thought about it, she had to admit, she was. Producer Katy Davis said, "I'll call you back in an hour." When she did, she said, "yes, you are." For two days a film crew from the Oprah Winfrey Show followed Kate Gladchun around HFM as she talked about all the deals and choices available. Soon after that she appeared on the show. The episode was entitled, "America's Smartest Shoppers." Kate Gladchun was one of them and her big find was Hickory Furniture Mart.[219]

In the meantime, Gladchun began her excursions, traveling to North Carolina on furniture buying trips for hundreds of shoppers. She handled the airfare, accommodations and which locations the group would visit. While they went to numerous stores, "up Highway 321 and beyond.... Fabric resources, places like that. However, we all agreed that the best deals to be had, the most helpful people and the greatest fun was

---

218   Email from Kate Gladchun to author, September 9, 2020.
219   Email from Kate Gladchun to author, September 9, 2020.

all under one roof – The Hickory Furniture Mart." One other advantage was the choices her shoppers were allowed with furniture they bought. Gladchun called it, "the best of both worlds." She explained, "outlet shopping for things that you knew you could use. But then, you could custom order, specify fabrics, trims, finishes, sizes and everything you could do at the Merchandise Mart in Chicago, The Michigan Design Center, and many of the other "To the Trade Only" places." For retail buyers who did not want to pay retail prices, HFM was heaven.

Kate Gladchun became Hickory Furniture Mart's most visible customer, bringing people from Michigan, but also New York, Florida, Minnesota, even California to Hickory. Stores stayed open late if her entourage needed extra time to look. If special sales were being held, the Gladchun group were alerted to those. Special meals were provided. But those who came also had their "mind blown!" by what they encountered. And the excitement wasn't limited to those Gladchun brought. As she described it, "I always walk into the Mart with excitement and hope. I KNOW I will find something new and exciting and "just right" for the current needs. Everyone always is more than happy to help, talented designers, interested in the latest project and not just in it for the sale. Hickory and North Carolina have some of the nicest people I have ever met." The relationship has been ongoing with dozens of trips under Gladchun's belt. She added, "Over the years, the Mart continued to grow, never disappointed and always seemed to reinvent itself for the needs of its customers. I love the smell, the sounds, the feel, the feeling of beautiful things to make a house a home." Her interest fit perfectly with the intent of the Mart to give everyone, including a guest on the Oprah Show the opportunity of a million choices in home decor easy and affordable.[220]

Greater interest by the buying public in furniture prompted Mart expansion of galleries to a number of outlets surrounding the main building, called "Shoppes at the Mart," part of the 40-acre complex on Highway 70. Nationally known furniture designer David Zagaroli, a Hickory resident, took his company, which fabricated his designs, to the Shoppes area to create a showroom offering the same kinds of discounts as seen in the Mart building. Touted as "top quality leather furniture," Zagaroli Designs constructed their pieces "of the highest-grade leather on kiln-dried hardwood frames" offering "30 colors and 26 styles." As Zagaroli himself put it, "in my 30 years as a furniture designer, I have been fortunate to have done some really good things." He added, "I decided that it may be good to bring some of these ideas in upholstery directly to the consumer."[221]

David Zagaroli began something of a trend. Soon, Leathermark, Inc. opened their "factory-direct showroom" at the Shoppes at the Mart too. With manufacturing facilities in Connelly Springs, in adjacent Burke County, owner/operator Charles Thornburg could load up his leather upholstery and send it right down Highway 70 (or Interstate 40) and be at his new showroom within a quarter hour. After that came Robert Bergelin Co., makers of custom European, American, and mission-style furniture.[222] Soon, Shoppes at the Mart hosted a wide array of furniture, not all of it for home interiors. Jo Ann and Larry Hollar opened Holiday Patio, sellers of "wicker, rattan and patio furniture by some of the leading names

---

220   Email from Kate Gladchun to author, September 9, 2020.
221   "Zagaroli Classics is open", CO, August 17, 1994, p. 5V; "Nationally Known Designer Opens Zagaroli Classics", October 30, 1994, p. 10Z.
222   "LeatherMark showroom", CO, August 28, 1994, p. 7V; "What's New", CO, October 3, 1994, p. 16D.

in the industry." The Mart had become a home furnishings mecca.[223]

Non-furniture business were also coming to the Mart. Grasso's Coffee House, opened at the Mart in the summer of 1994. Jeffery Grasso started with a location in Morganton and built his second location in the Mart. Coffeehouses were stirring new interest in and around Hickory with a number popping up around the same time as Grasso's. A year later, a full upscale dining experience for lunch and dinner was possible in the Mart as Jessica's offered "midday munching with a view." The restaurant offered 55 seats on Terrace Level One with "one side glass and the entire facility open to all levels of the building, which is built around an interior courtyard." With a continental breakfast spread, the eatery planned to add dinner service, said Jane Moore, who already had a presence in the Mart with Jessica's Porch Cafe.[224]

As the furniture industry changed, so did its products. Increasingly popular at the time was "motion-furniture," which featured "reclining chairs, sofas and other such items." One of the largest galleries for motion furniture in the Southeast opened at the Mart when the Comfort Zone occupied "8,000-square-feet of space on middle level three of the new four-story addition." The Comfort Zone joined Lexington Gallery, Century Clearance Center, Lane, Traditions France, and Waverly Place in the newly constructed section.[225]

Offerings left no stone (or home furnishings item) unturned. Besides antiques and designer fabrics, the Mart held space for sales of Oriental rugs, wall and floor coverings. Advertisements even said, "you'll

---

223 "Shoppes At Mart's Holiday Patio Sells Wicker, Rattan, Patio Items", CO, October 30, 1994, (Special Advertising Section), 6Z.
224 Shirley Hunter Moore, "A taste of the big city", CO, September 18, 1994, p. 1V; "Jessica's offers midday munching with a view", CO, April 30, 1995, p. 9V.
225 "Gallery at Furniture Mart", CO, December 25, 1994, p. 13V.

even go home with some exciting new lighting ideas." With heavy advertising in both the Charlotte and Asheville markets, newspaper copy drove home the point, "We're worth the trip."[226]

When the fall of 1995 rolled around it was time to take stock. Ten years earlier the Southern Furniture Market had picked up and left town. Everyone expected Hickory to suffer mightily from the withdrawal. Reporter Taylor Batten decided to take Hickory's temperature in the aftermath. The title to the October story said it all. "Vision Drives Hickory Empire Builder." The article focused on the man who changed the trajectory of Hickory from a furniture ghost town to a centerpiece. The report started with "this could have been an awfully bitter weekend for Leroy Lail." It was the weekend when "nearly 70,000 people were scampering around the International Home Furnishings Market in High Point." But instead of waving goodbye and anguishing over the loss, the article points out that Lail saw it coming, planned for the change and reinvented his Hickory Furniture Mart to cater to the retail market instead of the wholesale one. By that point, estimates were that over 400,000 people were spending in excess of $86 million within the walls of his vastly expanding complex.[227]

In seeing the changing nature of furniture buying, Leroy Lail planned wisely. He opened a series of hotels in Hickory, all near the Mart, invested in a number of restaurants on land he owned, and guided the City of Hickory to complete an $8 million trade center to diversify the reason people came to Hickory. But still the main reason for visitors was

---

226 "Disco er the Big Attraction in Furniture Shopping" (advert), Asheville Citizen-Times, May 21, 1995, p. 6.
227 Taylor Batten, "Vision Drives Hickory Empire Builder", CO, October 22, 1995, p. 1-7C.

furniture, thanks to his retooling of the Mart. With over 80% of visitors coming to buy furniture from outside the Catawba Valley, he had single-handedly revitalized Hickory and its economy. Not bad for a 25-year-old, just out of the Navy after four years at UNC-Chapel Hill who admitted he didn't know much about furniture when he took over management of the Mull's complex at the request of his father-in-law. As Batten mentions in the article, "nothing at the time indicated that the business contained the seeds of a multimillion-dollar business empire." And maybe Leroy Lail didn't know at the time he took the helm that it did, but he had confidence that he could make it work. Noting "the restaurant was known as much for flooding the basement showroom as for serving good food to its customers," (the basement is where the Furniture Mart began), Lail rolled up his sleeves and went to work. "As the showroom's manager, he did it all; scrubbed floors, picked up litter in the parking lot, and made sure the flooding stopped."[228]

By the early 80s the tea leaves were clear, but Leroy Lail was the only one reading them. Turning loss into gain, he guided the new Hickory Furniture Mart to an average growth of 18% per year, an astounding rate. As the article noted, "His success with the Furniture Mart translated into his other ventures." Some required aggressive moves, which he took, including the occasional criticism that went with them. But his contemporaries hailed his vision. Real estate developer Jim Tarleton said, "He's not shy when it comes to going after business," adding, "but I've never had an experience when he was unfair or dishonest." Hickory City Manager Gary McGee agreed, saying, "He's very aggressive, and most aggressive

---

[228] Taylor Batten, "Vision Drives Hickory Empire Builder", CO, October 22, 1995, p. 1-7C.

people come under fire." But as far as vision, McGee credited Lail with being able to think ahead of the pack. "Leroy does have a vision of the future of the area and he wants very much to be a part of it." As for Leroy Lail in his own words, he credits his analytical abilities and very much respects the lessons of history in a self-critique. "I would agree I'm hard-driving," admitted the then 56-year-old. He ended the article by modestly revealing, "I have some vision. And I get that vision through experience...I can see where we're going because I know where we've been."[229]

"The students have never been to America, so they've been impressed with the conveniences and choices available." That's how Lenoir-Rhyne professor Bob Simmons charactered the visit of five Russian foreign exchange students who came to Hickory to learn American business. Their tour of the Hickory Furniture Mart, along with other sites gave them a first-hand look at something quite different from the "planned economy" they were accustomed to back in the old Soviet Union, which had just ended four years earlier.[230] What the Russians saw in terms of furniture commerce was staggering, especially to a group who had never seen a market economy.

Not long after their visit, the Mart planned to ascend to even loftier heights. Announcing the fourth major enlargement of the Mart since its conversion to a public facility 11 years earlier, plans called for another four-story addition that would advance showroom space to 17 acres. The new area added to the total, now created "some 17 acres of professionally decorated showrooms under one roof."[231]

---

229   Taylor Batten, "Vision Drives Hickory Empire Builder", CO, October 22, 1995, p. 1-7C.
230   Shirley Hunter Moore, "5 Russian students get a taste of American business at L-R", CO, April 12, 1996, p. 5V.
231   "Mart's 4th and Biggest Expansion Is Under Way", CO, April 28, 1996, p. 3X.

Press continued to roll in from across the country about the Mart. A quote from the Los Angeles Times gushed that "it was at the Hickory Furniture Mart where we found the lowest prices for items on our shopping list," while in the New York Times, "the variety of merchandise at the Hickory Furniture Mart was spectacular." At that point, a directory of stores in the Mart took five pages.[232]

Within its own market, the Mart saw its share of competition. Since it started as a retail outlet, local furniture stores had always been an alternative to the the larger Mart with its variety and prices. Another furniture city just up the road from Hickory attempted the same plan. Lenoir, home to Bernhardt and Broyhill had seen its shopping mall decline after a few years of viability. Nearby manufacturers like Kincaid and Thomasville decided to bring their excess inventory there to offer to the public, ostensibly like the Mart. Said Eddie Kiser, Kincaid Outlet Manager, "This is an outlet for merchandise that we can't move, but we're not going to sell you a piece of trash." The idea never caught on and within a short period of time the Lenoir mart idea fizzled.[233]

A few years later the same attempt was made to take Hickory's Catawba Mall, a smaller indoor mall, (much like Lenoir's) and convert it into a furniture outlet. And much like Lenoir's effort the Catawba Furniture Mall did not have the longevity of the older, established Mart on the other end of Highway 70 in Hickory. The Catawba Furniture Mall, at less than half the floorspace of HFM, closed within a decade.[234]

New space in the Furniture Mart was not always being taken by

---

232 "What They're Saying About the Mart", CO, April 28, 1996, p. 7-15X.
233 Shirley Hunter Moore, "A shot in the arm(chair)", CO, September 18, 1996, p. 4C.
234 Andrew Shain, "U.S. 70: Fast growing at both ends", CO, February 6, 1997, p. 1, 12V; Shirley Hunter Moore, "In the market for furniture? You've come to the right place", CO, September 27, 1998, Where We Live Section, p. 26.

new tenants. Palliser, "Canada's largest maker of household furnishings," doubled its showroom space in the latest addition. To fill the square footage, Palliser planned to "add a line from Boyd, a California-based maker of bedroom furniture and TV/entertainment units, and expand its own line of casual dining furnishings, including smaller pieces for kitchen eating areas." Palliser's neighbors in the new addition included a Bassett Direct Gallery, Boyles, DonLamor, Hickory Park and Southern Designs. All were scheduled for occupancy in the spring of 1997.[235]

Another big expansion came from Hickory Park Furniture. They added galleries for C.R. Laine, and Rowe, plus got into patio furniture with an Outdoor Gallery that showcased wicker and rattan pieces. Hickory Park's Generations youth gallery tripled in size while its home office and motion furniture areas expanded too.[236]

If there was ever a time reminiscent of the old Furniture Market at Hickory Furniture Mart, it was likely to be during the fall, ironically enough when buyers used to come to town. During October and November the area's foliage turned from green to vibrant colors of yellow, orange and red, bringing out leaf watchers to the North Carolina mountains for spectacular vistas filled with vivid landscapes. Many people used the opportunity to kill two birds with one stone, stopping off in Hickory to look for some furniture, then heading up to the mountains to witness fall colors, all within one trip. With the Mart advertising an After Market Sale, the combination proved irresistible for many. The influx made sense to Ann McGough, Marketing Director of the Mart. "People are entertaining at home in the fall and winter, and they get that critical eye of wanting to

---

235 "Palliser to double size in expanded Hickory Mart", CO, October 23, 1996, p. 5V.
236 Joby Nahas, "Firm expands its showroom", CO, August 10, 1997, p. 12V.

get new things," she said, characterizing fall as a "heavy hitter" for the Mart. She said it was when summer shoppers started to get serious about purchases. One couple drove all the way from St. Louis, MO, another from New Jersey to enjoy the fall scenery and the discount prices.[237]

While 80% of the buying public were out-of-towners, Mart planners created events to keep the interest of local shoppers. In 1997, the first free "Design Expo" sought to help attendees enhance the look of their own homes with a variety of seminars and speakers. Alexandra Stoddard, a "design guru" who not only authored over a dozen books on the subject, she also hosted the HGTV series "Homes Across America." Stoddard appeared on television with a number of public figures including Oprah Winfrey. The schedule also included Kate Gladchun, the leader of the Michigan gang of power shoppers, to discuss "how consumers can become smart furniture shoppers." The expo held a "chair building demonstration" instruction on "how to buy leather," and a session on "decorative floral arranging." Said Ann McGough, "we even plan to include a seminar on the relationship between styles in fashion and furniture."[238]

The next year another dazzling array of speakers, with similar credentials guided area homeowners on how to improve their interior space. Discovery Channel's Christopher Lowell, whose "Interior Motives" program was the network's highest rated daytime show, offered "Seven Easy Layers to Building a Beautiful Room." Additionally, Larry Laslo, a mainstay on the QVC shopping channel presented "A Look at the New Look." The two headliners, along with a roster of other speakers filled seats for Design Expo: '98 with inspiration for those looking to enhance

---

237   Andrew Shain, "Color of Money", CO, November 3, 1996, p. 1,8V.
238   "Furniture expo to feature design and color experts", CO, January 18, 1997, p. 5E.

their homes.[239]

While in Hickory, Christopher Lowell chose to film several episodes of his show at the Mart. He used several showrooms to produce segments that aired in the fall on the Discovery Channel. The interior design star offered praise for the variety and quality of furniture, accessories and the like he found in Hickory to his national audience.[240]

One of Lowell's guests from his HFM segments was herself a homegrown star. Michelle Rosson appeared on a "Tricks of the Trade" segment, impressing viewers with her knowledge of furniture. As General Manager of HomeFocus, a store in the Mart, Rosson had spent her adult career in the business, first with Century Furniture, then as a leather buyer for Palliser. When Palliser opened its HFM gallery, Rosson was selected to manage it. All that led to the prestigious honor of being selected by her peers as "Retailer of the Year." Furniture World Magazine sponsored the award and when presented with the trophy, William Holland said she "burst onto the scene about five years ago and was determined to think outside the box." The industry had taken notice of the imaginative approach she took to presenting her store in Mart. "You walk into the average furniture store, and it's pretty boring," said E.L. Thomas, president of the Virginia-Carolinas Home Furnishings Representatives Association. But he asserted, "HomeFocus is not boring - Michelle's made it colorful and eclectic. She's also got fun items on the floor like pool tables, things you wouldn't normally see. She's added a fresh excitement and a lot of energy." Rosson's work in her corner of the Mart typified the surprises awaiting shoppers as they strolled through the varied displays,

---

239 "Nationally Known Designers Bringing Expertise to Mart", CO, May 10, 1998, p. 1X.
240 "Mart To Be Featured on Discovery Channel", CO, May 10, 1998, p. 12X.

by that time totaling over 17 acres and 900 lines of choices.[241]

The Mart regularly drew big names in the field of furniture and interior design. "The founder and head of the new Department of Furniture Design at Rhode Island School of Design, recently visited the Hickory Furniture Mart to see a Hickory Museum of Art exhibit," read one story about Rosanne Somerson, who had been a woodworker herself. She became an instructor at the Harvard Extension School in the 1970s. Eventually, she would go on to become president of the school she represented in 1998, when she came to Hickory. Her influential work in Studio Furniture (individually crafted pieces) was considered important to its development.[242]

The designer who redecorated rooms at the White House in Washington, D.C. during the Clinton Administration, Kaki Hockersmith served as the featured speaker for the 1999 Design Expo. Among the rooms she remodeled were "the Treaty Room and the first family's living quarters." Additionally she redecorated the Oval Office, Lincoln Sitting Room and "portions of the presidential retreat at Camp David."[243]

One important offshoot of the Design Expo was another event that focused more closely on leather. A series of workshops on leather care and education proved quite popular. The Leather Expo was free for anyone who wanted to come and learn more.[244] The Mart added more ways in which it served as a furniture education center to augment its function as a sales center.

---

241   Kiernan Kramer, "HomeFocus' Rosson honored as state's Retailer of the Year", CO, November 1, 1998, p. 4V; "See What's New…At the Mart" (advert), April 7, 1998, p. 2A.
242   Jason Savage, "Designer judges contest", CO, January 3, 1999, p. 4V; https://en.wikipedia.org/wiki/Rosanne_Somerson
243   "White House designer speaks today in Hickory", CO, January 23, 1999, p. 9E.
244   Elin Bell, "Learn leather care at 4th annual expo", CO, June 10, 2001, p. 15V.

The renovation coming to fruition in May of 1997 was not even complete before an announcement came of yet another addition. HFM planned to construct "another four-story addition," this one to be a "Suppliers Wing." John Schenk called it another "response to demand." He offered, "it will accommodate the need for additional office and sales space not only for suppliers now located in our building, but for those who have been waiting to get in." The new area planned to sport a new "restaurant and library bar."[245] VP Scott Lail went ever further about the addition, the third in six years. By this time, the eldest of the Lail children joined the company after an earlier stint with Wachovia Bank. He characterized each expansion as driven by the market. He said, "what prompted all those expansions in the '90s was the demand." With interest in becoming part of the lineup at HFM always at a premium, "we would get a list of up to 10 folks and that was usually when we started looking at another addition, dependent on who they were in the quality of things," said Lail, adding, "we didn't add onto the Furniture Mart speculatively, we normally had at least handshake agreements. Then before we started construction, we had signed leases."[246]

A number of innovations to enhance the shopping experience for customers were developed. The Mart handed out "digital pagers" (in the era before common cell phone usage) to "couples or groups who need to split up during visits." A "Mart Cart" helped folks get from one end of the complex to another including "Showplace Hickory" and Applebee's which was situated nearby. The service desk was enhanced to help buyers "find the items" they were seeking and "answer a myriad of other questions."

---
245   "Another Expansion Planned at Mart", CO, April 27, 1997, p. 4X.
246   Interview with Scott Lail, Hickory Furniture Mart, September 2, 2020.

Mart management continued to pay close attention to the bottlenecks that interrupted shopping and provide out-of-the-box solutions to those problems, to the benefit of all.[247]

By 1997, HFM was on the web. Acknowledging the experience might be new to some customers, ad copy read "if logging on is part of your regular routine, don't forget to drop in on the Hickory Furniture Mart's home page at http://www.webcom.com/hickory/." The instruction went on to read "if you are just surfing, you can find us by clicking on Travel and Tourism, North Carolina, Hickory, Furniture, Accessories and other topics." The new path to internet savvy consumers was just another way the Mart could attract prospective buyers.[248]

Eventually, the Mart pulled in all the local factories to sell their overruns, discontinued lines and and samples. In the summer of 1997, Hickory Chair, one of the city's oldest ongoing companies announced its intention to place an outlet in the Mart, its first. Both case goods and upholstery were part of the array that Hickory Chair offered at its new outlet.[249]

It seemed that the only thing that could slow down business was Mother Nature. In the summer of 1997, a landslide that caused closure of I-40 west of Asheville denied buyers west of North Carolina easy, interstate access to Hickory. In Asheville, officials estimated a 15-20% loss of business as drivers were forced to bypass not only Asheville but also Hickory down the mountain. Mart officials said they noticed a "slight drop" in their summer numbers. But the downturn did not hamper their annual

---

247   "Mart Guest Services Expanded" CO, April 27, 1997, p. 7X.
248   "Surf Us On The Net", CO, April 27, 1997, p. 15X.
249   "Hickory Chair opens first furniture outlet", CO, July 13, 1997, p. 6V.

Furniture Festival, its 11th which went on without a hitch.[250]

However, the popularity of HFM did not stop the entire area around it from substantial growth. A plethora of restaurants, retail chains and hotels all began to locate along the Highway 70 strip, near both the Mart and Valley Hills Mall. Traffic, even with the landslide, was tremendous, even stifling. The access road to the rear, named Catawba Valley Boulevard relieved some congestion but turns and progress on 70 were slow. The glut of traffic had prompted highway planners to construct a new road to connect Interstate 40 and Highway 70 less than a mile from where it was already established. Exit 126 (McDonald Parkway) became an answer to frustration behind the wheel, creating for HFM, a closer route to the Interstate than previously.[251]

One casualty of the expansion was one of the first "Shoppes at the Mart." After 11 years, Lynn Lail chose to close the Scarlet Butterfly. During the construction of the new interchange she said, "we had to live with orange cones for a long time." The disruption of traffic translated to a disruption of business. "It was hard to get in, hard to get out." But the space was not vacant for long. While announcing the closing of her women's clothing store she revealed that a "furniture-related business will soon move into the space."[252]

Even with the loss of the Scarlet Butterfly, the Mart had become a magnet for business. The Catawba Valley Visual Arts League had held exhibitions of their members work at HFM for years but when the organization decided to move their store, the More Art Gallery, they chose to locate adjacent to the Mart. Since the work of their artists had adorned an

---
250   John Goldberg, "I-40 slide hurts Unifour", CO, August 17, 1997, p. 1V.
251   John Goldbert, "Dinner dollars", CO, September 7, 1997, p. 1V.
252   Jennifer Rothacker, "2 fine-apparel shops are closing", CO, July 19, 1998, p. 16V.

uncounted number of homes stocked with furnishings from the Mart, the relocation seemed entirely logical.[253]

It didn't take much for the largest furniture clearance sale in North Carolina to be staged at Hickory Furniture Mart. After all, the resources, inventory and promotion to hold an event that outsized every other facility, not only in the Tarheel state but throughout the country was always within reach any time one was planned. A sale, billed as the biggest took place with the Mart's largest retailer, Boyles (which ran four showrooms in the Mart) leading the charge. From Baker to Thomasville, Boyles provided just one more reason for travelers to sojourn from long distances to see what the commotion was about.[254]

Businesses knew how to create excitement when the Mart proposed an all-encompassing sale. Palliser, now HomeFocus staged a "Dutch Auction" for one day only where they announced "prices drop 10% every half hour." The problem for shoppers was if they waited too late, hoping for the lowest possible price, everything would be gone. It was a power shoppers dream.[255]

Just after the HomeFocus Dutch Auction came the Labor Day celebration. It was like no other event ever staged at Hickory Furniture Mart. By that point the fifth, and largest addition was complete, populated and ready for even more customers. The opening of the "new South Atrium" pushed the floor space at the Mart to over one million square feet. The complex bested all other by containing a fifth floor. To mark the moment, gift certificates, game tickets for the Carolina Panthers, and gift baskets

---

253 "More Art has new place", CO, September 4, 1998, p. 8V.
254 "The Largest Furniture Clearance Sale in North Carolina" (advert), CO, July 31, 1999, p. 8A.
255 "Factory Authorized Dutch Auction", CO, August 4, 1999, p. 4V.

from Southern Living Magazine were all being given away.[256]

At that point, it was easy to get lost in Hickory Furniture Mart. Advertisers regularly posted the floor on which they were located to help customers find them. When Rhoney Furniture, one of the early tenants, expanded its showroom in the summer of 2000, it clearly posted the fact that it was "located on Level 2."[257]

Late in 2000, the economy of the Catawba Valley was measured by Sales & Marketing Magazine. What they found was staggering. When totaled, the cumulative amount of business being done in the four county Unifour area was $4.16 billion dollars. At the time, it equated to all the money ever made in the Star Wars franchise. The amount outpaced "tourist magnets like Asheville and Myrtle Beach." Residents were flabbergasted. A significant portion of that boom could be attributed to the Hickory Furniture Mart, with its expansion and sales that drew buyers from all over the country.[258]

When the Bank of Granite, a regional bank with 14 outlets sought to locate one of its ATMs at a site other than its own branches, the Hickory Furniture Mart was the first installation. The automated teller machine was the 15th.[259] The addition of an ATM on premises made transactions easier. The accessibility added another way in which HFM could consider its customers' needs in the buying process.

In September of 1999, the Mart welcomed Jane Earnest as Marketing Manager. Formerly with Valley Hills Mall, Earnest looked back, recalling, "I just knew I'd end up at the Hickory Furniture Mart some-

---

256 "The Mart Hits a Million" (advert), CO, August 28, 1999, p. A19; "Big addition at Furniture Mart", CO, August 29, 1999, p. 17V.
257 "Rhoney Furniture expanding", CO, July 2, 2000, p. 5V.
258 Adam Bell, "Catawba Valley is a retail powerhouse", CO, November 5, 2000, p. 9B.
259 "Bank of Granite ATM", CO, October 29, 2000, p. 13V.

day!" The reason? "My dad was in the furniture business in the 1960s and 1970s." While at the Mart, expansion reached all the way to Florida. In 2003, a second location opened in Fort Pierce at the intersection of two interstates. While it was a prime location and a good extension of the brand, Earnest recalls marketing the Florida Furniture Mart provided some obstacles, saying "not being there on a daily basis was definitely a challenge."

Jane Earnest might still be with HFM today were it not for another challenge that pulled at her heart strings. "I loved working at HFM but felt called to take over the Humane Society of Catawba County, which was struggling to raise money to build a shelter and spay/neuter clinic," said Earnest. A community agency supported often by the Mart, she left in 2005 but often found herself returning. "I visit the Mart often and what a testament to the good companies and good people that there are so many of the same employees are still working, some 20 years later," a testament to the positive work environment she found there, along with many of her colleagues. Recalling the experience, she looked back on her time fondly saying she "enjoyed working with Scott and Brad, Leroy and Lynn, and learned so much from my time there."[260]

About the time many furniture companies were offshoring production of their pieces, the Mart began a campaign to highlight those that did not. "Made in Carolina: Celebrating our Furniture Heritage" extolled the craftsmanship and value of home furnishing made within a short car ride from the Mart galleries. Reminding shoppers, "We're Worth the Trip," the Mart wanted to remind buyers about the value of American

---

260   Email communication between Richard Eller and Jane Earnest, August 31, 2020.

furniture at a time when many workers were being displaced.[261]

Another new campaign sought to highlight the continuous growth of retailers in the Mart. Under the banner of "Look What's New At The Mart!" changes were energetically reported. When David Zagaroli moved his Zagaroli Classics to a larger space in the Mart on Level One, the ad reported the move to demonstrate that the offerings within were ever changing and expanding. It became a good way to stay abreast of the growth that could lure shoppers back after they thought they had seen everything.[262]

By some accounts, the Mart had grown to gigantic proportions. One example was a column written by Charlotte Observer columnist Mary Canrobert. When she and her husband became empty-nesters, they decided the time was right to buy a new sofa, maybe a leather one. Like it did for many, the couple "thought we'd have a quick run-through at Hickory Furniture Mart to see everything in leather." Her next word was "Ha!" After an afternoon of shopping she admitted "there is no such thing as a quick run-through of that place." Acknowledging that her feet hurt from shopping, she experienced what almost anyone (without superpowers) feels after trying to see everything. It is just not possible in an afternoon, especially when one expects to just jaunt through.[263]

The Mart recognized the dilemma. Purported as one of North Carolina's "unique destinations," the building now housed 1000 lines of furniture. In addition to its standard "worth the wait" logo, advertisements now added "so much to see, you'll want to stay an extra day." The

---

261   "Made in Carolina" (advert), CO, February 21, 2002, p. 7X.
262   "Look What's New At The Mart!", CO, September 4, 2002, p. 2A.
263   Mary Canrobert, "Empty Nest? Add leather", CO, July 7, 2002, p. 1V.

experience of Mary Canrobert could be seen in the new tag line.[264]

The new millennium brought recognition of the status of HFM as a powerhouse in furniture sales. There was simply no other furniture outlet, store or mall to compete with the selection, savings and convenience of the Mart. It was reflected in its own advertising, which stated, "Hickory Furniture Mart is the largest facility of its kind in the nation and one of North Carolina's leading visitor attractions. Located at 2220 Hwy. 70 S.E., the million-square-foot complex has been featured in major publications and on top-rated TV shows. Nearly a half-million people visit the Mart every year."[265] Try as they might, other outlets did not compete with all the offerings of HFM.

In 2003, HFM announced its first Fabric Fair. The event focused on the selection and care of fabrics for home decorating. Seminars were held on aspects of available fabrics used in furniture, in a variety of events not unlike the earlier Leather Expo. Fashion coordinators helped those in attendance "offered tips on choosing fabrics to suit personalities and lifestyles." In addition, the Mart coordinated a sale that offered "5-20% off upholstery."[266]

The Fabric Fair also highlighted The Gold Leaf Club at the Mart. A new concept to reward repeat customers, the fair offered members the opportunity to "start earning Mart rewards." Soon, all advertising from the Hickory Furniture Mart reminded shoppers to "Ask about our Gold Leaf Club."[267]

---

264   "Unique Destinations", CO, March 15, 2003, p. 17A.
265   "Hickory Furniture Mart" (advert), CO, August 16, 2002, p. 12X.
266   "In other developments" CO, June 8, 2003, p. 11V; "Fabric Fair" (advert), CO, June 8, 2003, p. 18A.
267   "Fabric Fair" (advert), CO, June 8, 2003, p. 18A; "Hickory Furniture Mart" (advert), October 9, 2003, p. A3.

Just up Highway 70, Hickory's Family Guidance Center offered a variety of services to the community when needed, from individual counseling to domestic violence services. When the Center held a golf tournament to raise much needed funds, Hickory Furniture Mart was there as a "Leadership Sponsor." "Caring for families since 1958" was the motto of the Family Guidance Center, a United Way agency, and the needed support like that of HFM made "a difference in the lives of children and families and helped build a stronger community."[268]

Sponsoring important community events, HFM welcomed the PGA Champions Tour to Catawba County by sponsoring a full furniture pavilion. A tent at the 18th hole, displayed a range of home furnishings from stores within the Mart. Since HFM had become the area's most famous landmark, its presence at the PGA event seemed quite natural. To be sure, the "tent" was no spontaneous structure. It measured 50 x 70 feet, was air-conditioned, with a full floor. Placement was near both the putting green and driving range, so all the participants had easy access. No sales were transacted but "visitors can receive product information and discount coupons for various lines."[269]

The golf tournament, and HFM's sponsorship within it paid off substantially. Every year during the Greater Hickory Classic, many of the golfers' wives would visit the Mart and make purchases. In 2006, Judy Ahern "shopped to fill their Colorado pad" while husband Jim competed. No one talked numbers but Mart president Dwayne Welch called it "a substantial amount" of business generated by the PGA's arrival at the Rock Barn Golf Course. In terms of total impact, the event was responsi-

---

268   "Family Guidance Center", CO, August 10, 2005, p. 11V.
269   "Furniture Pavilion", Co, September 14, 2003, p. 4V; "Crenshaw, Zoeller join field at this week's Greater Hickory Classic", CO, September 21, 2003, p. 7V.

ble for an estimated $15.3 million in economic impact, well outstripping any other event that year in the Greater Hickory Metro area.[270]

Not only had Hickory Furniture Mart become "Hickory's most famous attraction," it was also becoming known to the world. Called "an international resource," stories of customers from abroad began to circulate. One such account revealed a staff member from a Mart store flew "to England to help a customer furnish a castle." Regularly, royalty from Saudi Arabia flew into Hickory to shop. The largest single furniture order, though, came from the United States. A $300,000 order went to Salt Lake City. With "some 100 factory outlets, stores and galleries in the complex" selling "more than 1,000 lines of furniture, accessories, rugs, art, wall coverings, fabrics and other furnishings," it was no surprise that people all over the globe were hearing about the deals. One source reported that the Mart's website averaged 3 million hits per month. Whether the site reached that number or not, the internet began to serve as an important component of marketing for HFM.[271]

The tastes of the world invaded the Mart as well. While attracting interest throughout the planet, a bit of the world of wider tastes came to the second level of the Mart when Santa Claire's Tearoom opened in the summer of 2004. Offering "Victorian English decor" and an array of teas from Harney and Sons, shoppers could also get scones and a selection of Irish foods. It seemed as HFM attracted the world, it also reflected it.[272]

Over the years, the Design Expo got more and more hands on with those looking to freshen the decor of their home. The 2004 event

---

270 Hannah Mitchell, "PGA event is an comic hole-in-one", CO, September 26, 2006, p. N10.
271 "Hickory Furniture Mart Is Internationally Famous", CO, August 15, 2003, p. 12X.
272 "Buy furniture, and stop for cup of tea", CO, August 8, 2004, p. 1V.

implored attendees to "bring a photo of your greatest decorating dilemma" to the January occasion.²⁷³ It was just another step in the process of helping educate the customer and bring them together with the retailers who could help them realize their dreams in home furnishings and decorating.

Always looking for innovative ways to accommodate the needs of customers, a Level 1 tenant, the Hickory Coffee Co. offered what it called at the time "an e-mail cafe." A phenomenon that later became commonplace, the trend was new at the time. So new, in fact that the amenity needed a bit of explanation. The announcement read "laptops equipped with a wireless card and are Linksys-compatible can surf the Web from the cafe." Anyone who might still be confused could call the Mart or go to the website for details.²⁷⁴

Hickory Furniture Mart had become a landmark in the community, complete with annual events. Consumers came to expect them. Art in the Mart came during the winter.²⁷⁵ In 2004, the Furniture Festival which had been a staple for almost two decades added participation in the Greater Hickory Classic golf tournament at Rock Barn to its roster of events.²⁷⁶ With all its space and promotional activity, even with the newer Leroy Lail built convention center, HFM drew people to its gatherings.

Occasionally though, a unique event popped up that blended art and commerce. "CURV-ITURE" sought to celebrate "furniture designed to incorporate curves." The exhibit was a cooperative project of the Mart, the Hickory Museum of Art and Hickory's Century Furniture. The goals

---

273   "Design Expo 2004", CO, January 5, 2004, p. 5A.
274   "Hickory Coffee Co. an e-mail cafe", CO, February 8, 2004, p. 3V.
275   "Art in the Mart" CO, February 13, 2004, p. 2V.
276   "Virginia woman earns VIP package", CO, September 1, 2004, p. 5V.

of the three organizations were the same. Under the umbrella of the "Furniture Society, a non-profit group that works to advance the art of furniture making," HFM, HMA, and Century Furniture supported efforts that highlighted the unique heritage of turning wood into furniture in useful but creative ways.[277] Always looking to cultivate public interest in the trends of society that drove consumption choices, Leroy Lail kept envisioning promotions that welcomed crowds to come see the latest.

The first decade of the new century found Hickory Furniture Mart always mentioned first among Hickory's attractions. A Raleigh, NC, travel writer venturing to Hickory warned readers, "don't be surprised if you spend a day there." Remarking specifically on the superior service received, Nan Chase referred to her time there as an "excellent furniture shopping adventure."[278] She was referring to what had become "the biggest tourism draw in the Catawba Valley."[279]

"Famous" was now the way the press characterized Hickory Furniture Mart. One notice in the Raleigh News and Observer, highlighting trips for North Carolinians asserted, "It's an easy drive to Hickory and the famous Hickory Furniture Mart. Tour nearly a hundred showrooms packed with famous brands of home furnishings and ideas galore." For any tourist, in state or out, a stop at HFM was mandatory, whether they needed furniture or not.[280]

The recognition that the Mart brought also shown light on its leaders. Lynn Lail was appointed to the North Carolina Citizens for

---

277 "Opening reception for CURV-ITURE", CO, September 30, 2004, p. V2.
278 Nan Chase, "To market, to market", News & Observer (Raleigh), March 7, 2004, p. H1, 7.
279 "Catawba: Enjoy the great outdoors", CO, September 26, (Living Here Section). p. 45.
280 "NC Piedmont", News & Observer (Raleigh), October 20, 2004, p. 8.

Business and Industry, "the state's largest business group."[281] Leroy Lail, after serving on the board of trustees of Hickory's Lenoir-Rhyne College went on to donate his time and expertise to a number of state government committees culminating with a seat on the University of North Carolina Board of Governors, which oversaw the 17 campus UNC system. It was a homecoming of sorts for the man who took over the Hickory Furniture Mart in 1963. UNC-Chapel Hill was his alma mater.[282]

The Lail's became sought after for their expertise and experience in the business of furniture and other ventures. Lynn Lail served as a Catawba County Commissioner for three, four year terms.[283] During her tenure, she was interviewed by CNN for its "Your Money" segment.[284] Speaking of CNN, Leroy Lail found himself on the bill with Lou Dobbs, then anchor of CNN's "Lou Dobbs Tonight." A forum in Raleigh, "The Political Economy," welcomed Dobbs and Lail to speak on the business climate in North Carolina. The event included about 400 state lawmakers and was held at the North Carolina Museum of History.[285]

It was something of a Lail family dynasty that was being established. Son Scott Lail was appointed to the N.C. Banking Commission, while Brad was a member of the Hickory City Council. Both sons were vice-presidents of Hickory Furniture Mart.[286]

Advertising for the Mart was plentiful. Besides ads placed by HFM itself (which included television spots), individual stores within also

---

281   Tom Murphy, "Landis elected to NCCBI board", Rocky Mount Telegram, April 19, 2004, p. 1,2.
282   Leroy Lail, "Win-Win", Redhawk Publications, 2020'; "Haywood County man named to UNC Board", Asheville Citizen-Times, April 4, 2007, p. 3.
283   "Results", CO, November 6, 2002, p. 15A.
284   "Washburn", CO, July 31, 2009, p. 5E.
285   News & Observer (Raleigh), June 12, 2005, p. E2.
286   "Lail reappointed to N.C. bank panel." CO, October 9, 2005, p. V12;

advertised regularly. But those notices were not the only way folks found out what was going on inside. Regularly, events showed up in places like the "Arts Calendar." For example, "Designing an Opportunity: Studio Furniture in the American Furniture Industry" was highlighted as a culturally interesting activity that drew interested persons to the Mart to hear a panel discussion connected with the "Curt-iture exhibit" going on at the time. The discussion included a number of furniture celebrities brought to the area by HFM.[287]

Bringing talent to the ears of Mart attendees was not a one-time thing. In early 2005, HFM announced "weekly seminars," scheduled for every Saturday at noon, which welcomed a variety of experts for seminars at "Santa Claire's Tearoom on Level 2." Topics ranged from "What's New in Patio Furniture" to "How to Choose a Rug to Match Your Furniture." The sessions were free to the public but as usual, space was limited.[288]

The spirit of giving back to the community, which had always been a part of HFM's personality, also infected many of the store owners within. In the spring of 2005, when a showcase of home decor benefited "A Child's Place, the Charlotte program that provides school and other support for homeless children and their families," the Mart's tenants Hickory Park and DonLamor helped out. Angie Allen, Angie Wright and Elizabeth Burns of Hickory Park and Donna Chamberlain of DonLamor took on the job of creating stunning interior designs for the Union County home.[289]

Sometimes the Mart served as the middleman in helping the community. When Hickory artist Danny Robinette "donated a painting to

---

287 "Arts Calendar", CO, November 12, 2004, p. 9V.
288 "Design Expo", CO, January 11, 2005, p. V3.
289 Allen Norwood, "Feel that warm glow inside", CO, March 10, 2005, p. H1.

benefit Family Guidance Center," HFM "volunteered to sell the painting for the center, which will receive all proceeds." It was a way for both artist and HFM to come to the aid of the Family Guidance Center which was going through "funding cutbacks affecting the facility."[290]

Development around the Mart grew apace in the first decade of the 21st century. In addition to Catawba Valley Boulevard, which offered a southern entrance to the Mart, came a shopping center between the Mart and Valley Hills Mall, as well as a next, closer exit from Interstate 40. McDonald Parkway, named for longtime Hickory Mayor Bill McDonald, provided visitors a more direct path to HFM. Now, furniture shoppers looked for Exit 126 as they trekked to Hickory Furniture Mart from all over the state, the nation and the world.[291]

The new, more direct routes helped. When Hickory landed a conference of the N.C. League of Municipalities, expecting 1,700 participants, just about all of them came to a "welcome party" put on by Hickory Furniture Mart. The opening, with plenty of food and drinks, as well "as exhibits from all five counties" gave attendees plenty of opportunity to furniture shop prior to the proceedings. But more than that, the Mart invited the Hickory Jaycees to hold a fundraiser within the party to benefit the Humane Society of Catawba County where $2,500 was raised to "build a permanent no-kill shelter."[292]

The Mart served as a magnet in Hickory. When the already popular Cafe' Gouda was looking to open a third location in Hickory, it came

---

290   "Painting benefits guidance center", CO, March 24, 2005, p. V3.
291   Heather Howard, "What's in store for the new year?" CO, January 1, 2005, p. 5B: "Latest", CO, June 26, 2005, p. 17V.
292   Jen Aronoff, "Hickory readies for gathering of hunters of state officials", CO, October 13, 2005, p. V1, 10; "Jaycees donate $2,500 to build permanent no-kill shelter", CO, December 9, 2005, p. 2V.

to HFM. Becca Phillips, one of the owners expressed excitement "about trying to be a positive fixture in the Hickory community, and we feel like the Furniture Mart is a big part of the history of Hickory and the future of Hickory." Taking over the space that was formally Jessica's Veranda, closing due to the retirement of Susan Abernathy, the new restaurant presented its full menu for furniture shoppers. Said Phillips, "We had this opportunity at the Mart, and we really want to run with it."[293]

Within a few years there was competition for eats at the Mart as another downtown Hickory restaurant added its menu for furniture shoppers. Taste Full Beans Coffeehouse, established a second location in the Mart at the south entrance. With "coffee, espresso, hot and cold drinks, smoothies, milkshakes, Hershey's ice cream, bakery pastries, loose leaf teas and local whole bean selections," the coffeehouse also provided WIFI access for the full experience.[294]

Taste Full Beans brought with it, its own art celebration. For ten years, Aroma of Art held an art show at its location in downtown Hickory. With the creation of a second location, the event for art lovers moved to the Mart. In addition to various pieces for sale, the show also supported a local charity, picking different ones annually, This year, the "non-profit receipts" went to Flynn Home, a "residential recovery program for men," the Women's Resource Center, and ALFA (which the Mart had supported for years).[295]

It's true that Hickory Furniture Mart brought local furniture to

---

293 "Cafe Gouda at Furniture Mart", CO, November 17, 2005, p. 7N.
294 "Taste Full Beans", CO, October 26, 2008, p. 8V; "Taste Full Beans Coffeehouse and Taste Full Arts Gallery", Hickory Furniture Mart: The Magazine: 47th Buying Guide Edition, p. 65.
295 Betty Stone, "Aroma of Art head to new location this year", CO, January 8, 2012, p. V2.

the world, but regularly it also brought the world to Hickory. The "Artful Living Gallery" in 2006 presented the creations of Yarek Godfrey a noted artist from Poland who lived in Paris. He garnered numerous "gold medal" awards and was featured "in New York, Las Vegas, Warsaw, Paris and Montreal." The popularity of featured artists such as Godfrey inspired the gallery to feature painters each month as part of a series. The list included artists from near and far.[296]

After several earlier attempts, the Mart established permanent Sunday hours in 2006 to meet "longstanding customer demand." According to then Marketing Director Tracey Trimble, the move paid off from its very first Sunday. "The tenants were very, very happy and very surprised we had such a big turnout on our first Sunday," she revealed. Previously, the Mart had only held Sunday hours during special events. Now, the first few Sundays were 'extra special' with music by the Catawba Valley Community Show Choir featured one week and artists from Winston-Salem presenting a "demonstration and trunk sale" the next.[297]

Hickory Furniture Mart also invested heavily into the success of the city and county that surrounded it. When the Catawba County Economic Development Corp. kicked off its new "Committee of 100, a campaign to recruit more private money to support efforts to lure jobs and investment," the Mart was a sponsor, along with other community businesses like Duke Power, Shortage, Alex Lee, and both hospitals, Catawba Valley and Frye Regional medical centers. The support created opportunity for marketing, business recruitment, analysis, site and part development efforts." Naming their dream "Project Bullseye" the group

---

296   Casey Childers, "Artful Living gallery at Mart", CO, December 29, 2005, p. V3; "Watercolorist's works on exhibit", CO, May 18, 2006, p. V3.
297   "Furniture Mart open on Sundays", CO, January 13, 2006, p. V3.

would eventually see the seeds of this effort come to fruition when Park 1764 (later renamed Trivium) was announced, to be located one mile south of the Mart building.[298]

Not only the Mart itself, but the complex around it had become very popular for furniture sales. In August 2006, the Mitchell Gold + Bob Williams Factory Outlet opened in a "newly renovated space just west of the Mart building. The outlet moved after an eight year stint across town from the Mart. The new facility expanded its "product range, which now includes wooden furniture in addition to its mainstay upholstered items." The 16,000 square-foot showroom planned to add "pottery and other accessories" to round out the space. The move to the Mart was somewhat prompted by "several calls a week" to Marketing Director Tracey Trimble, asking about the availability of Mitchell Gold + Bob Williams furniture. According to Trimble, that led to "successful negotiations" to bring the store to the Mart complex.[299]

The effort to help people create better living spaces continued to progress as the Mart created a "Design Your Life" symposium. With a more internet savvy approach, HFM coached customers to first go to their website and investigate the "room planner feature" before visiting. Once folks devised their "personal floor plan" they were then encouraged to come to the Mart where "design consultant stations will be set up throughout the Mart, where people can receive advice from professionals affiliated with the American Society of Interior Designers and the Interior Design Society." The event offered chances to win "a complementary full day of interior design services from Sally Bentley of Designing Women,

---

298 "Committee of 100 reception", CO, March 24, 2006, p. V6.
299 "Furniture outlet moves next to mart", CO, August 20, 2006, p. 3V.

as well as a design-themed gift basket." Many of the Mart's stores also participated with incentives.[300]

Sally Bentley has referred to the furniture professionals, all part of the Mart's array of stores and services as a "family." She remembered when she first joined the family back in the mid-80s. "I incorporated Designing Women in 1984 and we did health care and hotel design." Bentley charactered the enterprise as small, "only about half as big as it is now." Those were the days before HFM expanded, explained Bentley. "That whole back south end was not built, and we would go over there and spec out product for jobs. So that's how we used it as a resource for our company."[301]

Within a decade, Designing Women moved from "contract design into more residential design" and decided it was time to move into the Mart since Bentley and her colleagues were spending so much time there. Then her business grew rapidly, to the point that her company has done work in every state in the Union, plus ten foreign countries. Designing Women uses the resources of all the other stores in the Mart to find just the right pieces for their customers. "We're independent," she asserted. "We don't belong to anybody. And yet, for us, it's having all of those resources so everybody benefits."

The range of options benefits her clients significantly. Shopping for the customers' tastes, as well as their budget, Sally Bentley's Designing Women takes all the work out of furniture buying for clients. She encourages them to enjoy the experience, wanting those who use her services to see the vast selection at Hickory Furniture Mart. "We do a lot

---

300 "'Design Your Life' weekend", Asheville Citizen-Times, September 26, 2006, p. 23.
301 Telephone Interview with Sally Bentley, September 2, 2020.

of work overseas and they all fly here. There's just too much to see. My thing is I want you to have the best time you can have when you're with me, and then I can make your house look good. But I want them to come here, it's an experience that should be fun."

One important point that Sally Bentley wants her clients to see is that choices can be as wide as the Furniture Mart itself. "We shop all over the building. We're not married to anybody. I think that makes it nice, so it's not like we're trying to sell you something to make some money off of it. Most every time there's lots of stores involved every day." For decorating professionals, HFM remains unique. Bentley added, "there's no place with 23 acres of furniture under one roof."

During her time, Sally Bentley has outfitted countless houses. It is a successful formula, working with Mart stores to find just the right pieces. As a result, repeat business has been inevitable. "We have been doing this so long that we did the big house for people 37 years ago. Then we did their downsize, then we did their children's houses. We have been wedding gifts to people. We have been like new home gifts to people, and now we're doing their grandchildren's houses. We know the family for years, for years and years and years."[302]

As a full service design shop, Designing Women works closely with not only the stores that sell the furniture, but also with the shippers. "A lot of times we'll fly in to meet the trucks or drive in to meet the trucks wherever they happen to be," said Bentley. "We do the installation, we have our own drapery installers that travel with us, wallpaper people that travel with us. We can go in and do a turn key, everything. When you come home, all you got to do is bring your toothbrush and just lay

---

[302] Telephone Interview with Sally Bentley, September 2, 2020.

down."[303]

As far as the family aspect to Hickory Furniture Mart, Sally Bentley has gotten to know many of the folks at the stores she shops. She loves them and has made the point that many are just about all of the companies at the Mart are family and/or locally owned. Designing Women does not make their selections at big box stores. The working relationships have gone well beyond the nine-to-five workday. She noted, "our kids all grew up together, we all see each other socially. It's a really cozy environment. I think that's very, very important, and people feel that when they come. They love to be in there."[304]

As another longtime observer of the "family" at the Mart, Scott Lail, in his more than thirty years professionally associated with the Mart, has seen the synergy of helping customers allow individuals to grow and shine. As he puts it, "A lot of folks that have gotten their career started at the Mart have done really well in the furniture business, in terms of other jobs that they've taken on." He calls HFM "a breeding ground" for innovation.[305]

Perhaps the best example of good customer service leading to a whole new type of job was Teresa Thompson. From 1986 to 1992, Thompson served as manager of Mull's Motel. During that time and after, Leroy Lail involved her in "various projects" connected to Hickory Furniture Mart. In 2003, what she calls "a simple request" turned into another career for her as Mr. Lail asked her to assist a hotel colleague who was moving from New York to a new home in Atlanta. "He needed an entire house full of furniture, didn't have a lot of time, and didn't know where to

303   Telephone Interview with Sally Bentley, September 2, 2020.
304   Telephone Interview with Sally Bentley, September 2, 2020.
305   Interview with Scott Lail, Hickory Furniture Mart, September 2, 2020.

start," she remembered. "Mr. Lail asked me if I would be willing to meet with this gentleman and take him around to each showroom inside the Mart to help him find exactly what he needed." She said she was "more than happy to help." Thompson spent two full days, trekking down everything the client had on his list to fill his new residence.[306]

  The shopper was so pleased with his experience that he relayed his satisfaction to Leroy Lail, and the Personal Shopper Program was born. The customer told Lail that "he could have never accomplished everything without the additional help and the personal shopping service that was provided to him." From that point, requests began to come in regularly from furniture buyers (often out of state) that needed multiple rooms furnished and had little time to shop. Thanks to Teresa Thompson, "today, Hickory Furniture Mart has turned personal shopping into a permanent service for its customers who are needing to furnish three or more rooms of their home during the same visit." She first discussed the need of the customer by phone, getting an idea of the styles and items for which they are looking, then she arranges a meeting at the Mart, where she guides them through the many showrooms "to find the exact styles, brands and price points that they are looking for while they are here." Once selected, Thompson handles logistics like shipping to make sure that all the customer has to do is go to the new house and enjoy the decor they have selected. As Thompson relayed, "it's always a thrill to see happy shoppers leaving the Mart after their successful furniture shopping excursion!" Her work has paid off with many satisfied customers who have enjoyed their time at Hickory Furniture Mart.[307]

---

306 Email from Teresa Thompson to Tracey Trimble, September 1, 2020.
307 Email from Teresa Thompson to Tracey Trimble, September 1, 2020.

Among the many innovations, the internet also gave HFM the chance to create its own competition with the "Extreme Room Makeover Challenge." With the public invited to watch at "www.hickoryfurniture.com" and vote for "the contestant most in need of an extreme room makeover," the competition rivaled a number of television shows where contestants vied for prizes. In this case, one "winner will receive select furniture pieces and one day of complementary design services." Voting was conducted online. Displays could also be seen at the "Carolina Home and Garden Show" at the Hickory Metro Convention Center. At the end of the show, Gray and Debbie Nester of Fort Mill, SC were announced the winners.[308]

By 2007 it was generally acknowledged that Hickory Furniture Mart was the "largest retail center of its kind in the nation." The "100 factory stores, outlets and galleries" was unmatched and continued to top the list of reasons why people came to Hickory. The website, now a standard mention in all advertising, was a stop before traveling to see the wide variety of offerings to get some idea of what to look for in a planned visit.[309]

There was good reason for coming to the Mart any day, now seven days a week, but still the After Market Sale, though the Southern Furniture Market itself had been gone to High Point for many years, remained a highlight. In her column "Living Here: Your guide to the Charlotte Region," Leigh Dyer wrote in October of 2007, "this week is a great time to tap into North Carolina's status as a furniture capital." She used the After Market Sale to promote the Mart, its convenience and its savings to her

---

308   "Extreme room makeover finalists", CO, March 4, 2007, p. 11V' "Hickory Furniture Mart winners", CO, April 19, 2007, p. H2.
309   "Furniture bargains found all around region", CO, September 30, 2007, p. Z62.

readers.[310]

The words "furniture" and "North Carolina" had become linked, creating a long and admirable history of the industry in the Tarheel state. One newcomer to NC wanted to know "why?" In their "News for Newcomers" series the News & Observer sought to explain the emergence of furniture making, saying that the title of "Furniture Capital of the World" began in the 1980s but the industry itself went back a century earlier. The answer admitted that "globalization and free trade took their toll on the industry from the 1990s onward," but called out by name Hickory Furniture Mart (also providing the website) as the place for the largest After Market Sale anywhere. "There one can find 100 factory outlets, stores and galleries representing 1,000 furniture manufacturers."[311]

Tourism might not seem like an industry driven by furniture but Hickory Furniture Mart had made it so. Visits by the furniture buying public translate not only into sales at HFM but the ancillary benefit to Hickory of hotel stays and restaurant visits. Long a part of the legacy of furniture production in the Catawba Valley, the City of Hickory has gone so far as to feature the tradition in its promotional campaign, using the slogan, "Life, Well Crafted."[312]

Beyond its name recognition all over the world, HFM pulled people to Hickory, especially those relocating in the Southeast. Vice President Brad Lail recalled back in the early years of the 21st century adding a "marketing arm to go up to the mountains and talk to the realtors and developers up in that area." Al Priest served as a liaison that helped build-

---

310 Leigh Dyer, "It's a capital opportunity for furniture shopping", CO, October 26, 2007, p. D1.
311 Lamara Williams-Hackett, "News for Newcomers", News & Observer, October 29, 2007, p. 12.
312 https://www.hickorync.gov/life-well-crafted-brand-and-partnership-information

ers take the next step to creating an inviting home for potential buyers by furnishing, through HFM the houses they built. The effort worked beautifully. According to Lail, "there were so many people that were relocating from other states and just making sure that they had our buying guide information, that they had materials when new home buyers were talking to them that they could share with them. So that was a pretty big."[313]

Fall proved the busiest time of the year for Hickory Furniture Mart. Then, Marketing Director Tracey Trimble, in addition to her work at the Mart, kept "a close eye on the changing colors" every autumn." During the season, Trimble submitted "a leaf report for www.visitnc.com." Her observations on the "magnificent reds and yellows" in the foothills alert visitors of what they would see in the foothills when traveling there. She also knew it was good marketing. With the already popular After Market Sale, leaf watchers would likely stop in to also watch sale prices. "Many of them plan their trips (shoppers) around the fall color," she observed.[314]

Tracey Trimble, who now serves as Executive Vice President and General Manager, weathered more than autumn colors in her job as marketing director. When the Swedish furniture company, IKEA came to Charlotte, creating such a sensation among likely furniture buyers, she had done her research and was undeterred. Noting that many of the Mart's customers were "baby boomers looking for more traditional furniture" she responded to press questions about competition. "Our demographics are so different from that there's definitely a niche for both."[315]

As ubiquitous as it had become, it was no surprise that Hickory

---

313   Interview with Brad Lail, Tracey Trimble, Hickory Furniture Mart, August 27, 2020.
314   Daniella Lopez, "WCNC: Your Weather Connection", CO, November 3, 2007, p. 6D.
315   Jen Aronoff, "IKEA opens, says it can weather economic storm", CO, February 19, 2009. p. 2V.

Furniture Mart also became a campaign stop. In 2008, Chelsea Clinton toured the facility to promote her mother, Hillary Clinton's campaign for president, during the state's primary. She came to Asheville, and Winston-Salem, making one stop in between in Hickory, at the Mart.[316]

In 2010, Hickory Furniture Mart celebrated its 50th anniversary. During that summer, Mart officials wanted to show their appreciation to the customers who came in droves to visit and buy. For an entire week, the Mart gave every customer who walked through the door and bought $2,000 worth of furniture a $50 gift card for gas. [317]

Leadership of Hickory Furniture Mart had always been a prime focus of Leroy Lail's. Perhaps more so than his other business interests, the success of the Mart demonstrated his abilities to build, promote and manage. So when Lenoir-Rhyne (now) University put together a series called "Aspects of Leadership," his observations on what it took were absolutely imperative to the discussions. Along with the heads of CommScope, Hickory Springs and SunTrust Bank, Lail offered advice based on his many years of leading a business, one that had become phenomenally successful.[318]

Among the many events hosted by Hickory Furniture Mart, perhaps the hardest to pronounce was "the Region 13 Piedmont meeting the International Phalaenopsis Alliance." As it turns out, Phalaenopsis is a type of orchid and the Catawba Valley Orchid Society sponsored the event. Orchid growers were there to show and sell their plants, as well as answer questions. There were a number of speakers talking about everything

---

316   Mike McWilliams, "Chelsea Clinton in WNC today", Asheville Citizen-Times, April 27, 2008, p. 1.
317   "Celebrate 50 yers with a $50 Gas Card" (advert), CO, June 20, 2010, p. 1.
318   "The Lenoir-Rhyne University Business", CO, September 4, 2011, p. L6.

from Taiwan Phalaenopsis to a session entitled, "Phalaenopsis: A Journey of Imagination."[319]

Given that orchids had ties to home decor as an accessory, there was no subject too far for the Mart to tackle when it came to furnishings. One admonition pleaded, "don't leave your furniture naked." The 13th annual "Slipcover Summit" was coming to HFM in the summer of 2012. With professionals presenting on techniques of their sewing skill, the summit offered folks the opportunity to "network and make their own furniture slipcovers."[320]

Just as HFM had always been a good community citizen, supporting worthy causes with its time, its facility and its resources, management encouraged its tenants to do the same. One vitally worthy cause centered around one man, Donald Hicks. After teaching for years in the Charlotte-Mecklenburg School System and seeing what students did not have when they came to learn, he decided to act. With the help of his wife Dana, he began Classroom Connections, a resource for both students and teachers. He took it upon himself to find the paper, pencils and other materials necessary for successful learning. Appealing to every company he could think of, he approached "the Light Place at Hickory Furniture Mart." They, along with other businesses donated. Each summer, a flock of teachers invade space provided by Bethel United Church of Christ to gather supplies for the coming school year. For them, everything is free.

Most folks would not think furniture production has much to offer "poor children" in school but Donald Hicks disagrees. In an interview he pointed to a "bolt of white fabric." He said, "You know when cheerlead-

---

319 "The Catawba Valley Orchid Society will", CO, January 8, 2013, p. V4.
320 Rebecca Horoschak, "Home Notes", CO, June 16, 2012, p. H3.

ers run out before a football game with those large banners? Those cost close to $50. We can supply yards of this fabric - which they can write on - for free." The philanthropy generated by the Mart and its tenants help the community in ways largely unseen. But the ethic is there.[321]

Over the years, shops have come to the Mart, and while some have closed, each has provided a story that reveals the opportunity that comes in an association with the Hickory Furniture Mart. Among those was Kim Sigmon, who seems to have furniture in her blood. If she does, it came at an early age when she remembers "the sound and smells" of the factory where her father worked as an upholsterer at Ethan Allen Furniture, in the Catawba County town of Maiden. She took what would turn out to be a lifelong interest that in 1998 would result in "The Lion's Den Interiors," a continuing part of the Mart's designer offerings. Combining her father's work and her mother's "passion for fine furniture and a deep love for lion statues," Kim Johnston-Ingle opened her business at HFM, specializing in "unique products that set her store apart from everyone else."[322]

Rick Grant is another example of an individual who possessed a love of furniture and experience in the industry, leading him to very successful operations within Hickory Furniture Mart. Rick and his wife DeDra opened the Hooker Furniture Outlet in 2009. They quickly expanded to four stores inside the Mart. Two years after first jumping in to retailing at HFM, Grant opened Heritage Furniture Outlet. Soon he acquired "Southern Style Fine Furniture and also opened Heritage Furniture Gallery and Clearance Center."[323]

---

321   Skip Marsden, "Busy man gets busier creating supply resource for educators", CO, October 14, 2013, p. B2.
322   "The Lion's Den Interiors", Hickory Furniture Mart: The Magazine: 47th Buying Guide Edition, p. 19.
323   "Heritage Furniture Galleries", Hickory Furniture Mart: The Magazine: 47th Buying

Growth has been generational for Giovanni Guidi. Since opening his Reflections Furniture with his wife Natalie in 1985, concurrently when the Mart was transitioning to retail, the couple has grown the company, which features leather upholstery significantly. They have also grown a family of four daughters who are now "taking their family business to the next level and exposing a new generation to everything their father and mother worked so hard to create." Their business model also looks to the future as they plan to teach "their own children about the business, cultivating a third generation" of furniture retailing, all within Hickory Furniture Mart.

A strong family tradition is at the heart of many paths taken to Hickory Furniture Mart. Some extend all the way down to the High Point. Helen Starnes and her husband Ralph started with a paint and wallpaper company in the 1940s. It wasn't long before they began designing spaces for furniture at the High Point Market. From there, granddaughter Sally McEachern felt the influence of both her mother and grandmother to study design and create "Designing Women," a design firm that offers full service and tasteful decor to a wide range of clients. The company quickly gained acclaim after helping Catawba Memorial Hospital with a "$14 million renovation project," where they designed the "hospital's first birthing center along with their emergency room and MRI and oncology centers." Since then, Sally McEachern-Bentley and her associates regularly help those who need an expert eye to furnish their own homes. Designing Women help take the stress out of furniture buying by offering ideas that avoid "costly mistakes" that save consumers both "time and money."[324]

Guide Edition, p. 46.
324   "Destined for Design", Hickory Furniture Mart: The Magazine: 47th Buying Guide Edition, p. 14.

It looks as though all furniture roads lead to Hickory Furniture Mart. That is certainly the case for one of Hickory's long standing retailers. The Hudson family has been selling furniture in the area for over a century. With stores in Connelly Springs and downtown Hickory, Lindy's Furniture had become a staple with furniture buyers. But Katie Hudson-Purgason "had a vision to expand." She opened "Simplly Home by Lindy's" in 2004, located inside HFM. Still a family enterprise, Hudson-Purgason said, "we've always stayed true to our values from day one." She believes her grandfather "would be proud of the way we have honored his legacy." She insists that customer's of Lindy's Furniture be treated like family, adding that "if we treat them well, they will come back year after year."[325]

The business of selling furniture can be a daunting proposition. But not for Monique Dunn. After a career of jetting the globe, presenting "high-end jewelry" to both wholesalers and retailers, Monique took on the challenge of selling the same type of clientele on a different commodity. in 2004, she started with 3,000 square feet in High Point, hoping to add a second location in Hickory. When space became available in the Mart, she recruited her son Jason "to join her as a partner," eventually moving her entire operation to Hickory. Now with over 11,000 square feet at HFM. Her "premier leather" offerings include "a wide variety of American Made" leather furniture in a very successful operation.[326]

Just like the way many furniture manufacturing companies got their start in the 1960s, 70s and 80s in the Catawba Valley, so too did fur-

---

325   "Celebrating 101 Years and Four Generations of Selling Furniture", Hickory Furniture Mart: The Magazine: 47th Buying Guide Edition, p. 44.
326   "Leather and More", Hickory Furniture Mart: The Magazine: 47th Buying Guide Edition, p. 54.

niture retailers. Eddie Bumgarner began his career in one of those factories until he decided to sell furniture rather than build it. With his cousin Ronnie, Eddie began buying pieces from "a handful of Amish builders." They told others what a pleasure it was to work with the Bumgarner boys and soon Amish Oak and Cherry expanded to a second location at Hickory Furniture Mart. Just like many other companies, Eddie brought in his daughter Misty to manage the store at HFM. Misty's husband Jeremy is now also part of the organization that specializes in products that "strongly support American builders, manufacturers and their families." And with twin grand-daughters Charleigh and Sadie, Eddie believes that one day, they will indeed take over the company he started.[327]

Hickory Furniture Mart has bred success for many of its retailers. Good's Home Furnishings, from a small footprint in 2009 in the Mart, has grown to five locations, four of them still in HFM. Randy Good and Scott Lever just recently celebrated their tenth anniversary at HFM. Cultivating "solid relationships" with manufacturers, some locally well-known, the two North Carolina men have grown a very successful operation that includes, by their own admission, "the best seasoned team in the industry."[328]

The business of furniture spawns a number of other types of companies, directly related to home furnishings that have found a home at HFM. One unique offering is Roya Rugs. David Mostafaloo began his store as "Unique Oriental Rugs & More By David" in a tiny 700 square foot space in 2004. After realizing he had a passion for everything asso-

---

[327] "Amish Oak and Cherry", Hickory Furniture Mart: The Magazine: 47th Buying Guide Edition, p. 56.
[328] "Good's Home Furnishings Celebrates Their 10-Year Anniversary", Hickory Furniture Mart: The Magazine: 47th Buying Guide Edition, p. 43.

ciated with the process of rug making, he started the business to offer his knowledge to customers looking to enhance their furniture purchases at the Mart. The business succeeded exponentially. Mostafallo's enthusiasm rubbed off on his son Saman, who joined the business and now designs rug creations for his generation, millennials, to put in their homes. Color, design and anticipating styles years in advance are what keeps the father and son owners closely attuned to the choices made by their customers.[329]

The process of making an Oriental rug is extensive. As many as 300,000 knots might be tied in the construction of one rug, depending on size. "Craftsmen spin multiple yarns into one," to create unique colors. Patterns range from traditional that have been used for centuries to something new like the designs Saman Mostafallo creates. Roya Rugs, like many of the other stores in the Mart, offer products that are singular, a collection of which any shopper would not find anywhere else in the world.[330]

Another company that took something of a winding path to Hickory Furniture Mart was Resource Design of Hickory. Larry Spierer worked as a special education teacher in Miami. His wife Jaye was a flight attendant for Delta Airlines. The only connection they had to Hickory was a small company owned by Larry's mother and step-father in Conover, called Regency Home Fashions. The company sold fabrics, some to well-established companies like J.C. Penney, Sears and Fingerhut. But in the 1980s, Larry's mother Terry thought that "Hickory Furniture Mart needed a really good fabric store." She and her husband Lou started

---
[329] "Igniting a Passion For Rugs", Hickory Furniture Mart: The Magazine: 47th Buying Guide Edition, p. 39.
[330] "Hand Knotting", "Spinning of the Wool", Hickory Furniture Mart: The Magazine: 48th Buying Guide, 60th Anniversary Edition, p. 42-43.

Resource Design of Hickory in the late 1980s, and by the early 90s, Larry Spierer's mother had convinced him and his wife to join the company. Tragically, Terry Silver passed away shortly after her son and daughter-in-law came to Hickory. Larry and Jaye Spierer were asked to "step in and help run Resource Design, a job they have had for 30 years now.[331]

Along with Taste Full Beans, a number of restaurants have delighted customers, store personnel, and the community with scrumptious food. When Cafe' Gouda left the Mart to concentrate on its restaurant in Hickory, an opening appeared for an accomplished father and son catering team to expand their business, as restaurateurs. Chuck Spaller and his son Jordan accepted the challenge, opening The Wooden Spool Cafe in 2012. Offering an assortment of fare, Chuck relied on his more than 40 year's experience in food preparation. Jordan, following in his dad's footsteps graduated from Johnson & Wales University to add to the cuisine in new and interesting ways. Among the many popular favorites is the sour cream potato salad. The Wooden Spool Cafe has become a destination in itself for folks both local and out-of-the-area.[332]

Perhaps the most vital but least considered business for an operation like Hickory Furniture Mart is shipping. J & L Furniture Services handles the job for Hickory Furniture Mart, with expert handling of newly purchased furniture for shipping to homes across the state. Juan Rodriguez has over 40 year's experience with not only handling furniture but also its restoration. Along with his son Luis, they provide the much needed service of delivery for stores throughout the Mart. With such expertise,

---

[331] "Resource Design of Hickory", Hickory Furniture Mart: The Magazine: 47th Buying Guide Edition, p. 50.
[332] "The Wooden Spool Cafe", Hickory Furniture Mart: The Magazine: 47th Buying Guide Edition, p. 64.

J & L have been called upon to restore home furnishing pieces that has suffered abuse, everything from neglect to pet stains. Juan and Luis Rodriguez are another multi-generational team that keep the pace of activity going at HFM like the well-oiled machine it has become.[333]

Just as these services suggest, sometimes furniture buyers need assistance in picking out and placing just the right piece in their homes. One expert who has helped clients do just that is Angie Cline. Her word for Hickory Furniture Mart is "AMAZING." In working with the Mart for over fifteen years, she touts the vast resources contained within that often blow her clients away with the selection and quality they find. According to Cline, "We have the luxury of bringing clients to one location for several days and having them preview thousands of manufacturers at one time prior to purchasing. The showrooms all have the newest market selections of fabrics, finishes, and furniture pieces."

The selection found at the Mart offers the opportunity to go so far as to take one piece of furniture from a store and match it with a separate piece from another. The selection is that large and when asked where else can a shopper do that, Angie Cline has another one word answer. "NOWHERE!" Looking back to the way it once was done, Cline remembers, "prior to this resource, most designers had to rely on photos of furniture pieces and small fabric snips to present to the client and hoped they liked it. While a picture is worth a thousand words, there is nothing better than allowing the client to see a furniture piece in person, touch it and feel the fabrics to solidify the decision."

Angie Cline appreciates all the help from store personnel in

---

333   "Shipping Your Furniture Home Safely Consolidated Shipping Provided by J&L Furniture Services", "J&L Furniture Services", Hickory Furniture Mart: The Magazine: 47th Buying Guide Edition, p. 66-67.

helping connect buyers with the right furniture, pieces they will derive satisfaction in owning. "Everyone at the HFM goes out of their way to help the designers and our clients," points out Cline about their contact with HFM. "They literally bend over backwards to make sure our customers feel like royalty and the experience is one they will fondly remember forever." She has observed that people talk glowingly about the experience of shopping, not a common occurrence. While much of that is a tribute to the help offered by sales associates at the many stores they visit, Cline also acknowledges the atmosphere created by the Lail's in making sure that everything from security to the clean, tasteful environment they encounter. A true testament to the world customers walk into when they enter Hickory Furniture Mart, Cline, only half jokingly, admits that "some of our clients just want to move into HFM and never leave!"[334]

The shutdown of gatherings that accompanied the coronavirus pandemic of 2020 has been devastating for businesses across the country, but less so for the Mart. As HFM Vice President Brad Lail pointed out, "Had we not had the foundational pieces built already and up and running, lead generations and all that, it would have been a much more difficult time for us." Because of the work done to promote the Hickory Furniture Mart brand online, the Mart was well positioned to accommodate non-contact inquiries. Says Lail, "we saw a surge in traffic during COVID. People were home, they were looking about their homes and we've continued to see surge in traffic and leads and all that. We have invested in the systems to capitalize on that."

Sally Bentley agrees. Designing Women has seen a boost in business during the coronavirus pandemic, instead of a downturn. She

---

[334]   Email communication between Angie Cline and Richard Eller, September 1, 2020.

noticed, "It is amazing to me in the last probably two months, we have been busier since March than we have been since, I can't tell you when. We were slammed, it is unreal, work everywhere. But it is amazing to me that they only want products made in America. I'm like, "Yes, that is perfect." We can absolutely supply it, I love it."[335]

Creating the online presence of HFM goes back to those days when the organization got a website early, but it goes much deeper than just a URL. Brad Lail noted the website "became a place for customers to learn about the Mart to plan their visit, and it still is that. But now we've made significant investments and enhancements. The website is a more integral part of what we are doing here at the Mart." Mart stores have come to depend upon the umbrella of support and promotion that brings traffic, either in person or online to see the product each store features. It has changed the way many shop.

For many furniture shoppers, there's nothing like kicking the tires, so to speak. Brad Lail put it this way, "people still want to look, see, sit, feel." But with customization and a new generation of furniture shopper, the online presence has created many more opportunities for buyers to get exactly what they want. The analogy of buying furniture to that of a car purchase is apt for Lail who sees a great similarity in the process. "Buying patterns are changing as the younger group becomes more comfortable in an online environment," he asserts. "It used to be that a person buying a new car would walk into four or five different car dealerships before they bought. Now when they're ready to buy a car, they go to one dealership because they've done all the work online. We think that that's somewhat true with regards to the furniture."

---

[335] Telephone Interview with Sally Bentley, September 2, 2020.

In the last 60 years, leadership at the Mart has paid strong attention to the needs and buying patterns of furniture shoppers. Those observations have led to innovative ways HFM has anticipated trends well into the future. Those innovations kept the Mart going, even prospering when everyone around them were fretting over the loss of one market, not seeing what the Lail's and their team was seeing, the creation of another, even stronger market. Brad Lail sees beyond HFM's 60 years, betting on where it will go from here. He notes, "the brand value has grown beyond just the brick and mortar location of this and where it all happened and has been happening for 60 years. That's begun to translate into the online environment. So folks, when they see our name they generally associate positive things with it." But he does not discount the rich heritage that built the complex where the brand recognition was built. He added, "they've heard about the Mart because of its history. We've worked hard to build a high level of trust with those customers, which in turn benefits the showrooms here in the building, directly.

As the umbrella under which billions of sales have been conducted, the name "Hickory Furniture Mart" has served as a funnel to help customers find the furniture they are looking for in the stores that are located within. Technically, HFM does not sell furniture to the public, but it has created a climate through its website to assist people in seeing what is available, and ultimately helps them to buy. Hickory Furniture Mart represents 100 stores that currently offer approximately 1,000 manufacturer brands to the public. Being a part of such a positive brand with a strong identification among consumers that drives traffic and sales is what defines Hickory Furniture Mart as a leader in the industry. "It benefits everybody," says HFM VP Brad Lail. "All the products are available for viewing. If somebody finds something they want, they request information, they immediately are contacted. It's an automatic process. Their showrooms are notified and they take it from there."

As a major component of continually bringing people to Hickory, the Mart has stayed very involved in the tourism industry. Vice President and General Manager Tracey Trimble announced that Hickory was awarded the "travel and tourism convention" to be held in March of 2021. As Trimble reveals, "all travel and tourism industry professionals are coming" to see the City of Hickory showcased. In the age of COVID, with tourism a vulnerable industry, the convention, expecting to bring up to 700 attendees, might look somewhat different from gatherings of the past, but the selection signifies the importance of Hickory Furniture Mart to putting Hickory on the destination map for so many travelers.[336]

But the process becomes more high tech, there remains no substitute for old-fashioned, personal contact. One proven aspect to the continuing reputation of the Mart is word of mouth. As Vice President and General Manager Tracey Trimble noted, "the largest amount of our customers have either shopped here before, or they've been referred by friends and family. So that's where that reputation comes in. We get a lot of people that say, 'Oh, if you need something in Hickory...' or, 'my mom bought her bedroom set here when she first got married.' We hear that all the time."

For folks who travel, saying one came from Hickory is shorthand for both furniture and HFM. When in New York City, Tracey Trimble was

---

336   Interview with Brad Lail and Tracey Trimble, Hickory Furniture Mart, August 27, 2020.

asked the age old question, "Where are you from?" When she told them, the questioner immediately blurted out, "Oh, furniture." Since she was connected with the Mart, it was no surprise that her response was "I'm so glad that's the first thing you think of when you think of Hickory," not knowing her connection to HFM.[337] Colleague Scott Lail has had the same kind of incident, saying "I've been out traveling in different parts of the country and when I mentioned that I'm from Hickory, North Carolina, usually one of the first words out of their mouth is, "Oh yeah, furniture." As Vice President of Hickory Furniture Mart, he is gratified to hear that people equate his hometown with the product he works every day to promote.[338]

Tracey Trimble represents the level of talented people the Lail family has brought to the Mart to work with them in building the brand, now known all over the world. Trimble has been with HFM for a quarter of its existence, celebrating her 15th anniversary in 2020. She characterized her experience at the Mart as "an incredible opportunity these past 15 years to work alongside some of the most amazing and talented individuals and leaders within the furniture industry." Crediting the Lail family for sharing "their knowledge, insight and continued visions for growth," Trimble has watched "the furniture industry and the Mart transition and adapt to so many changes along the way." She continued, "I have gained such an appreciation for the vision that Leroy had from the very beginning and have always remembered to follow his remarkable advice of using every perceived challenge as an opportunity to make something better." Her pride in the work done to keep the Mart on top, along with her

---

337   Interview with Brad Lail, Tracey Trimble, Hickory Furniture Mart, August 27, 2020.
338   Interview with Scott Lail, Hickory Furniture Mart, September 2, 2020.

colleagues is evident. As good as the past has been, she eagerly anticipates the future, saying, "I look forward to seeing what lies ahead for the Mart and the furniture industry in the years to come."[339]

Likewise, Mandy Hildebran has worked closely with the Lail family for many years and has seen the reputation of Hickory Furniture Mart grow. It suits her work at the Hickory Metro Convention Center, also built by Leroy Lail. The Hickory Metro Convention Center took over some of the community events that HFM sponsored during its history, especially in the 70s and 80s, before the Convention Center was built. As director of the facility, Hildebran has studied what has brought people to Hickory. Often, the answer has a familiar ring to it. "Furniture is why many visitors come to our area and we always enjoy talking with people from throughout the nation and world when they stop in the Visitors Center at the Hickory Metro Convention Center." Noticing that many visitors have done their research before they travel, she observed that many "come to Hickory to go to the Hickory Furniture Mart because they are ready to purchase furniture made by local craftsman that will last a lifetime and longer."[340]

In addition to furniture shoppers, HFM provides an amenity that attracts others who come to the city as well. Said Hildebran from her perspective at the Hickory Metro Convention Center, "It's also an attraction which meeting planners see as a positive and often times Hickory is chosen to hold a conference because of the Hickory Furniture Mart. Meeting planners organizing a conferences also look at the community and what there is to do so attendees enjoy their time after a day of seminars at the convention center. We are fortunate to have a well-known furniture

---

339   Email from Tracey Trimble to author, September 3, 2020.
340   Email from Tracey Trimble/Mandy Hildebran, September 7, 2020.

shopping amenity in our own backyard."[341]

As Hickory Furniture Mart celebrated its 60th anniversary, it offered "Free shipping and shipping discounts on qualified purchases, during the month of March 2020. That happened to be the beginning of the coronavirus pandemic that swept across the world. As times have gotten tough in retail and mask wearing has become a necessary part of the culture, Hickory Furniture Mart has continued to look for appropriate ways to do business and continue its growth into the future.[342] The Mart's investment in technology and internet access have allowed it to weather the pandemic, creating a safe environment to buy furniture.

It has been an eventful sixty years. Nothing in that time has stayed the same, except for the fact that people are still looking for quality furniture to furnish their homes. Styles have changed, shopping opportunities have changed, prices have changed and even the way consumers think about outfitting their homes has changed. Certainly, Hickory Furniture Mart looks substantially different from its beginnings. From 6,000 square feet to over a million, from a wholesale only showroom to housing a thousand, HFM has gone from a small operation, almost an after thought, to the leader of a second industry in furniture production, that of retail sales.

Many thought when Hickory lost its hold on a portion of the semi-annual North Carolina Furniture Market, the town was through as a name synonymous with furniture making. Leroy Lail said 'not so fast.' He had a vision that could take such a change, a disaster as many saw it, and turn it around. He did so in spectacular fashion. Building and promoting.

---
341 Email from Tracey Trimble/Mandy Hildebran, September 7, 2020.
342 "60th Anniversary 1960-2020" (advert), CO, March 15, 2020, p. A17.

Proving that bad news did not have to be a death sentence. When he saw the furniture industry pivoting toward High Point, he pivoted too. In addition to the Mart, Leroy Lail has been instrumental in the development of hotels in our area including, Crowne Plaza, Best Western, Fairfield Inn, Courtyard by Marriott, Hampton Inn, Hilton Garden Inn, Holiday Inn Express and Holiday Inn Express & Suites. Hickory is the area from where he came and still chooses to live. To his credit, he created not only a whole slate of viable businesses, but also has helped them succeed beyond anyone's wildest imagination. Anyone's except his.

www.ingramcontent.com/pod-product-compliance
Lightning Source LLC
Chambersburg PA
CBHW020934090426
42736CB00010B/1136